LINUX™
FOR
DUMMIES®

Quick Reference

by Phil Hughes

IDG
BOOKS
WORLDWIDE

IDG Books Worldwide, Inc.
An International Data Group Company

Foster City, CA ✦ Chicago, IL ✦ Indianapolis, IN ✦ Southlake, TX

LINUX™ For Dummies® Quick Reference

Published by
IDG Books Worldwide, Inc.
An International Data Group Company
919 E. Hillsdale Blvd.
Suite 400
Foster City, CA 94404
www.idgbooks.com (IDG Books Worldwide Web site)
www.dummies.com (Dummies Press Web site)

Library of Congress Catalog Card No.: 97-080871

ISBN: 0-7645-0302-2

Printed in the United States of America

10 9 8 7 6 5 4 3 2 1

1P/RX/RS/ZX/IN

Distributed in the United States by IDG Books Worldwide, Inc.

Distributed by Macmillan Canada for Canada; by Transworld Publishers Limited in the United Kingdom; by IDG Norge Books for Norway; by IDG Sweden Books for Sweden; by Woodslane Pty. Ltd. for Australia; by Woodslane Enterprises Ltd. for New Zealand; by Longman Singapore Publishers Ltd. for Singapore, Malaysia, Thailand, and Indonesia; by Simron Pty. Ltd. for South Africa; by Toppan Company Ltd. for Japan; by Distribuidora Cuspide for Argentina; by Livraria Cultura for Brazil; by Ediciencia S.A. for Ecuador; by Addison-Wesley Publishing Company for Korea; by Ediciones ZETA S.C.R. Ltda. for Peru; by WS Computer Publishing Corporation, Inc., for the Philippines; by Unalis Corporation for Taiwan; by Contemporanea de Ediciones for Venezuela; by Computer Book & Magazine Store for Puerto Rico; by Express Computer Distributors for the Caribbean and West Indies. Authorized Sales Agent: Anthony Rudkin Associates for the Middle East and North Africa.

For general information on IDG Books Worldwide's books in the U.S., please call our Consumer Customer Service department at 800-762-2974. For reseller information, including discounts and premium sales, please call our Reseller Customer Service department at 800-434-3422.

For information on where to purchase IDG Books Worldwide's books outside the U.S., please contact our International Sales department at 415-655-3200 or fax 415-655-3295.

For information on foreign language translations, please contact our Foreign & Subsidiary Rights department at 415-655-3021 or fax 415-655-3281.

For sales inquiries and special prices for bulk quantities, please contact our Sales department at 415-655-3200 or write to the address above.

For information on using IDG Books Worldwide's books in the classroom or for ordering examination copies, please contact our Educational Sales department at 800-434-2086 or fax 817-251-8174.

For press review copies, author interviews, or other publicity information, please contact our Public Relations department at 415-655-3000 or fax 415-655-3299.

For authorization to photocopy items for corporate, personal, or educational use, please contact Copyright Clearance Center, 222 Rosewood Drive, Danvers, MA 01923, or fax 508-750-4470.

is a trademark under exclusive license to IDG Books Worldwide, Inc., from International Data Group, Inc.

About the Author

Phil Hughes is President of Specialized Systems Consultants (SSC) and publisher of *Linux Journal* magazine. He has authored or edited many of SSC's Pocket Reference cards for the UNIX operating system and utility programs.

Phil has worked in computing as a programmer and design specialist since 1968. He has worked with UNIX since 1980 as a systems programmer, consultant, trainer, and writer. In 1983, armed with that one English class he took in college, Phil turned SSC into a company that specializes in documentation for UNIX systems.

ABOUT IDG BOOKS WORLDWIDE

Welcome to the world of IDG Books Worldwide.

IDG Books Worldwide, Inc., is a subsidiary of International Data Group, the world's largest publisher of computer-related information and the leading global provider of information services on information technology. IDG was founded more than 25 years ago and now employs more than 8,500 people worldwide. IDG publishes more than 275 computer publications in over 75 countries (see listing below). More than 60 million people read one or more IDG publications each month.

Launched in 1990, IDG Books Worldwide is today the #1 publisher of best-selling computer books in the United States. We are proud to have received eight awards from the Computer Press Association in recognition of editorial excellence and three from *Computer Currents*' First Annual Readers' Choice Awards. Our best-selling *...For Dummies®* series has more than 30 million copies in print with translations in 30 languages. IDG Books Worldwide, through a joint venture with IDG's Hi-Tech Beijing, became the first U.S. publisher to publish a computer book in the People's Republic of China. In record time, IDG Books Worldwide has become the first choice for millions of readers around the world who want to learn how to better manage their businesses.

Our mission is simple: Every one of our books is designed to bring extra value and skill-building instructions to the reader. Our books are written by experts who understand and care about our readers. The knowledge base of our editorial staff comes from years of experience in publishing, education, and journalism — experience we use to produce books for the '90s. In short, we care about books, so we attract the best people. We devote special attention to details such as audience, interior design, use of icons, and illustrations. And because we use an efficient process of authoring, editing, and desktop publishing our books electronically, we can spend more time ensuring superior content and spend less time on the technicalities of making books.

You can count on our commitment to deliver high-quality books at competitive prices on topics you want to read about. At IDG Books Worldwide, we continue in the IDG tradition of delivering quality for more than 25 years. You'll find no better book on a subject than one from IDG Books Worldwide.

IDG BOOKS WORLDWIDE

John Kilcullen
CEO
IDG Books Worldwide, Inc.

Steven Berkowitz
President and Publisher
IDG Books Worldwide, Inc.

Eighth Annual Computer Press Awards ≥ 1992

Ninth Annual Computer Press Awards ≥ 1993

Tenth Annual Computer Press Awards ≥ 1994

Eleventh Annual Computer Press Awards ≥ 1995

IDG Books Worldwide, Inc., is a subsidiary of International Data Group, the world's largest publisher of computer-related information and the leading global provider of information services on information technology. International Data Group publishes over 275 computer publications in over 75 countries. Sixty million people read one or more International Data Group publications each month. International Data Group's publications include: ARGENTINA: Buyer's Guide, Computerworld Argentina, PC World Argentina; AUSTRALIA: Australian Macworld, Australian PC World, Australian Reseller News, Computerworld, IT Casebook, Network World, Publish, Webmaster; AUSTRIA: Computerwelt Osterreich, Networks Austria, PC Tip Austria; BANGLADESH: PC World Bangladesh; BELARUS: PC World Belarus; BELGIUM: Data News; BRAZIL: Annuário de Informática, Computerworld, Connections, Macworld, PC Player, PC World, Publish, Reseller News, Supergameprover; BULGARIA: Computerworld Bulgaria, Network World Bulgaria, PC & MacWorld Bulgaria; CANADA: CIO Canada, Client/Server World, ComputerWorld Canada, InfoWorld Canada, NetworkWorld Canada, WebWorld; CHILE: Computerworld Chile, PC World Chile; COLOMBIA: Computerworld Colombia, PC World Colombia; COSTA RICA: PC World Centro America; THE CZECH AND SLOVAK REPUBLICS: Computerworld Czechoslovakia, Macworld Czech Republic, PC World Czechoslovakia; DENMARK: Communications World Danmark, Computerworld Danmark, Macworld Danmark, PC World Danmark, Techworld Denmark; DOMINICAN REPUBLIC: PC World Republica Dominicana; ECUADOR: PC World Ecuador; EGYPT: Computerworld Middle East, PC World Middle East; EL SALVADOR: PC World Centro America; FINLAND: MikroPC, Tietoverkko, Tietoviikko; FRANCE: Distributique, Hebdo, Info PC, Le Monde Informatique, Macworld, Reseaux & Telecoms, WebMaster France; GERMANY: Computer Partner, Computerwoche, Computerwoche Extra, Computerwoche FOCUS, Global Online, Macwelt, PC Welt; GREECE: Amiga Computing, GamePro Greece, Multimedia World; GUATEMALA: PC World Centro America; HONDURAS: PC World Centro America; HONG KONG: Computerworld Hong Kong, PC World Hong Kong, Publish in Asia; HUNGARY: ABCD CD-ROM, Computerworld Szamitastechnika, Internetto online Magazine, PC World Hungary, PC-X Magazin Hungary; ICELAND: Tolvuheimur PC World Island; INDIA: Information Communications World, Information Systems Computerworld, PC World India, Publish in Asia; INDONESIA: InfoKomputer PC World, Komputek Computerworld, Publish in Asia; IRELAND: ComputerScope, PC Live!; ISRAEL: Macworld Israel, People & Computers/Computerworld; ITALY: Computerworld Italia, Macworld Italia, Networking Italia, PC World Italia; JAPAN: DTP World, Macworld Japan, Nikkei Personal Computing, OS/2 World Japan, SunWorld Japan, Windows NT World, Windows World Japan; KENYA: PC World East African; KOREA: Hi-Tech Information, Macworld Korea, PC World Korea; MACEDONIA: PC World Macedonia; MALAYSIA: Computerworld Malaysia, PC World Malaysia, Publish in Asia; MALTA: PC World Malta; MEXICO: Computerworld Mexico, PC World Mexico; MYANMAR: PC World Myanmar; NETHERLANDS: Computer! Totaal, LAN Internetworking Magazine, LAN World Buyers Guide, Macworld Netherlands, Net, WebWereld; NEW ZEALAND: Absolute Beginners Guide and Plain & Simple Series, Computer Buyer, Computer Industry Directory, Computerworld New Zealand, MTB, Network World, PC World New Zealand; NICARAGUA: PC World Centro America; NORWAY: Computerworld Norge, CW Rapport, Datamagasinet, Financial Rapport, Kursguide Norge, Macworld Norge, Multimediaworld Norge, PC World Ekspress Norge, PC World Nettverk, PC World Norge, PC World ProduktGuide Norge; PAKISTAN: Computerworld Pakistan; PANAMA: PC World Panama; PEOPLE'S REPUBLIC OF CHINA: China Computer Users, China Computerworld, China InfoWorld, China Telecom World Weekly, Computer & Communication, Electronic Design China, Electronics Today, Electronics Weekly, Game Software, PC World China, Popular Computer Week, Software Weekly, Software World, Telecom World; PERU: Computerworld Peru, PC World Profesional Peru, PC World SoHo Peru; PHILIPPINES: Click!, Computerworld Philippines, PC World Philippines, Publish in Asia; POLAND: Computerworld Poland, Computerworld Special Report Poland, Cyber, Macworld Poland, Networld Poland, PC World Komputer; PORTUGAL: Cerebro/PC World, Computerworld/Correo Information, Dealer World Portugal, Mac*In/PC*In Portugal, Multimedia World; PUERTO RICO: PC World Puerto Rico; ROMANIA: Computerworld Romania, PC World Romania, Telecom Romania; RUSSIA: Computerworld Russia, Mir PK, Publish, Seti; SINGAPORE: Computerworld Singapore, PC World Singapore, Publish in Asia; SLOVENIA: Monitor; SOUTH AFRICA: Computing SA, Network World SA, Software World SA; SPAIN: Communicaciones World España, Computerworld España, Dealer World España, Macworld España, PC World España; SRI LANKA: Infolink PC World; SWEDEN: CAP&Design, Computer Sweden, Computing Sweden, Internetworld Sweden, it.branschen, Macworld Sweden, MaxiData Sweden, MikroDatorn, Nätverk & Kommunikation, PC World Sweden, PCaktiv, Windows World Sweden; SWITZERLAND: Computerworld Schweiz, Macworld Schweiz, PCtip; TAIWAN: Computerworld Taiwan, Macworld Taiwan, NEW VISiON/Publish, PC World Taiwan, Windows World Taiwan; THAILAND: Publish in Asia, Thai Computerworld; TURKEY: Computerworld Turkiye, Macworld Turkiye, Network World Turkiye, PC World Turkiye; UKRAINE: Computerworld Kiev, Multimedia World Ukraine, PC World Ukraine; UNITED KINGDOM: Acorn User UK, Amiga Action UK, Amiga Computing UK, Apple Talk UK Computing, Macworld, Parents and Computers UK, PC Advisor, PC Home, PSX Pro, The WEB, UNITED STATES: Cable in the Classroom, CIO Magazine, Computerworld, DOS World, Federal Computer Week, GamePro Magazine, InfoWorld, I-Way, Macworld, Network World, PC Games, PC World, Publish, Video Event, THE WEB Magazine, and WebMaster; online webzines: JavaWorld, NetscapeWorld, and SunWorld Online; URUGUAY: InfoWorld Uruguay; VENEZUELA: Computerworld Venezuela, PC World Venezuela; and VIETNAM: PC World Vietnam.   3/24/97

Author's Acknowledgments

My biggest thank-you goes out to my friends and coworkers at SSC who have managed to tolerate me for the last few months while I wrote this book.

I hope it isn't too geeky to thank LINUX and the vi text editor for making at least part of the job much easier. And, while I am thanking nonhumans, I would also like to mention StarOffice, an office suite for LINUX that, among other things, managed to get rid of a virus for me.

Now, for the humans: Victorie Navratilova prepared the section on pico, a program she knows well. My contribution to her life was to introduce her to vi. Maybe pico will become a thing of the past for her.

I would also like to thank the gang at IDG, with Nancy DelFavero spearheading the effort. She listened to me complain about Microsoft software, and still managed to get a book out of me. Thanks also to the copy editors Mike Simsic and Joe Jansen, and acquisitions editor Ellen Camm. A thank-you also to Peter Salus, the technical editor on this project.

One final person needs to be thanked, and that's Linus Torvalds. I have worked with computers for more than 30 years and enjoyed much of it, but computing (and drinking beer) became real fun thanks to Linus and the LINUX community that has formed around his work.

Publisher's Acknowledgments

We're proud of this book; please send us your comments about it by using the IDG Books Worldwide Registration Card at the back of the book or by e-mailing us at feedback/dummies@idgbooks.com. Some of the people who helped bring this book to market include the following:

Acquisitions, Development, and Editorial

Project Editor: Nancy DelFavero

Acquisitions Editor: Ellen Camm

Copy Editors: Joe Jansen, Michael Simsic

Technical Editor: Peter Salus

Editorial Manager: Mary C. Corder

Production

Project Coordinator: Regina Snyder

Layout and Graphics: Jane E. Martin, Drew R. Moore

Proofreaders: Rebecca Senninger, Christine Berman, Janet M. Withers

Indexer: Sharon Hilgenberg

General and Administrative

IDG Books Worldwide, Inc.: John Kilcullen, CEO; Steven Berkowitz, President and Publisher

IDG Books Technology Publishing: Brenda McLaughlin, Senior Vice President and Group Publisher

Dummies Technology Press and Dummies Editorial: Diane Graves Steele, Vice President and Associate Publisher; Mary Bednarek, Acquisitions and Product Development Director; Kristin A. Cocks, Editorial Director

Dummies Trade Press: Kathleen A. Welton, Vice President and Publisher; Kevin Thornton, Acquisitions Manager; Maureen F. Kelly, Editorial Coordinator

IDG Books Production for Dummies Press: Beth Jenkins, Production Director; Cindy L. Phipps, Supervisor of Project Coordination, Production Proofreading, and Indexing; Kathie S. Schutte, Supervisor of Page Layout; Shelley Lea, Supervisor of Graphics and Design; Debbie J. Gates, Production Systems Specialist; Tony Augsburger, Supervisor of Reprints and Bluelines; Leslie Popplewell, Media Archive Coordinator

Dummies Packaging and Book Design: Patti Crane, Packaging Specialist; Lance Kayser, Packaging Assistant; Kavish + Kavish, Cover Design

◆

The publisher would like to give special thanks to Patrick J. McGovern, without whom this book would not have been possible.

Table of Contents

How to Use This Book 1

How This Book Is Organized 2
Conventions Used in This Book 3
Need More Information? 3
Icons Used in This Book 4

Part I: Getting to Know LINUX 5

What Is LINUX? 6
Selecting a LINUX Flavor 7
Installing LINUX 9
Fixing Installation Problems 10
   Errors while booting from a floppy 10
   System gets hung up during the boot 10
   System says it's out of memory 11
   You get a "Cylinder > 1023" error message 11
   You get an "Unable to Mount" message 11
   Win95 made LINUX vanish 11
   You're having hardware problems 11

Part II: Understanding the Shell 13

Available Shells 14
Basic Directory Commands 14
Character Quoting 14
   Quoting an individual character 14
   Using the close-quote character 15
Command History 15
   Setting command history mode 15
   Using Emacs mode 16
   Using vi mode 16
Customizing the Environment 16
   Creating shell aliases 16
   Displaying environment variables 17
   Setting environment variables 17
   Setting shell editing modes 18
   Standard environment variables 19
Directory Naming Conventions 20
Directory Referencing 20
Files Associated with a Program 21
   Redirecting the files 21
   Connecting commands 21
   Redirecting command output 22

Redirecting command input 22
Redirecting error messages 23
File Naming Conventions 23
Pathnames 24
Shell Command Elements 24
Shell Variables 25
Special Characters 26
Startup Files 28

Part III: Common Shell Commands 29

Archiving, Converting, and Other File Manipulation 30
  cpio — Creating and restoring archive files 30
  gzip — Compressing and decompressing 32
  More compressed file utilities 33
  tar — Working with tar archives 33
  uuencode — ASCII encoding 34
  uudecode — Decoding ASCII encoding 35
  zcat — Listing files without decompressing 36
  zip and unzip — Working with zip archives 36
Creating Schedules and Timed Events 37
  at — Scheduling commands 37
  cal — Displaying a calendar 38
  crontab — Scheduling periodic events 39
File Management Basics 40
  cat — Displaying the contents of files 40
  Conventions using dash and double dash 42
  cp — Copying files and directories 42
  less — Paging through a file 43
  ls — Displaying filenames and information 43
  mv — Moving a file 45
Online Documentation 45
  info — Displaying GNU-style online documentation 46
  man — The Old Faithful of Documentation 46
  /usr/doc — Finding online documentation 48
Printing 48
  gv — Displaying PostScript files 48
  lpq — Examining the print queue 49
  lpr — Queuing print requests 49
  lprm — Removing queued print jobs 50
  pr — Formatting files into pages 51
Sorting and Searching 52
  find — Locating a file that meets
    specified characteristics 52
  grep — Looking for patterns in files 53
  locate — Finding files quickly 54
  sort — Sorting data 55

Using Attributes and Permissions 56
    chgrp — Changing the group of a file 56
    chmod — Changing file access permissions 57
    chown — Changing the owner of a file 59
    umask — Changing your default file creation mask 59
Working with Directories and Disks 60
    cd — Changing directories 60
    df — Displaying free disk space 61
    du — Showing used disk space 61
    mkdir — Creating new directories 62
    pwd — Displaying the current directory location 63
    rmdir — Removing an empty directory 63
Working with File Content 63
    file — Describing the contents of a file 63
    fmt — Adjusting line lengths 64
    head — Displaying the first part of files 64
    ln — Creating multiple names for a file 65
    rm — Deleting files 66
    tail — Accessing the last part of files 67
    wc — Counting words, lines, and characters 68
Working with the System 68
    exit — Leaving a shell 68
    finger — Checking up on users 69
    mount — Mounting filesystems 70
    passwd — Changing your password 71
    ps — Checking up on the system 71
    su — Assuming another identity 72
    top — Monitoring system status 73
    w — User and system status 73

Part IV: Using X/FVWM **75**

An Introduction to X 76
    The Window manager 76
    The X client 76
    The X server 76
The FVWM Desktop Anatomy 77
    Applications windows 77
    The Pager 78
    The root window 79
    The Task Bar 79
Adding Backgrounds 79
Checking Out Programs under X 79
    gv — display PostScript files 80
    ical — appointment calendar 80
    xbill — video game for LINUX 80
    xcalc — desk calculator 80

xeyes — watching the MouseCursor 80
xmag — magnifying glass 81
xman — display man pages 81
xterm — terminal window 81
    Copying and pasting an xterm 81
    Exiting an xterm 82
    Scrolling through the xterm scrollback buffer 82
    Starting an xterm 82
xv — graphics displayer and manipulation tool 82
Examining Pull-Down Menus 83
    Applications menu 83
    Games menu 84
    Hosts menu 85
    Lock Screen menu 85
    Multimedia menu 85
    Preferences menu 85
    Screensaver menu 86
    System Utilities menu 86
    Utilities menu 87
    Window Operations menu 87
Exiting X 88
Modifying Window Characteristics 89
    Closing a window 89
    Destroying a window 89
    Maximizing a window 89
    Minimizing a window 89
    Moving a window 90
    Resizing a window 90
    Sticking/unsticking a window 90
Mousing with X 91
Moving around the Screen 92
Starting Applications 92
Starting X 92
Switching Tasks 93
Using Button Bars 93
Using Keyboard Shortcuts 94

*Part V: Text Editors and Working
with Text* *95*

Choosing an Editor 96
Editing Text with joe 96
    Checking out joe commands 97
    Exiting joe 98
    Getting help 98
    Searching for text 98

Starting joe 99
What else joe does 99
Editing Text with Pico 100
Checking out Pico commands 100
Exiting Pico 100
Importing a file into an edit session 101
Maneuvering around a file 101
Starting Pico 101
Editing Text with Emacs 102
Checking out Emacs commands 102
Exiting Emacs 103
Starting Emacs 104
Editing Text with vi 104
Defining vi modes 104
Deleting text 104
Exiting vi 105
Inserting text from other places 105
Recovering from a mistake 106
Repeating commands 106
Replacing text 106
Sample 107
Saving vi settings 108
Searching for text 108
Sample 109
Setting options 109
Starting vi 110
Using Input mode 110
Using operators and objects 111
Sample 112
Wrapping lines 112
Formatting Text with fmt 114
LINUXspeak.. 114
Sample 114
Formatting Text with groff 114
LINUXspeak.. 115
Sample 116
Spell-Checking with ispell.. 116

Part VI: Sending and Receiving E-Mail... 119

Collecting All the Pieces 120
Decoding MIME Messages with munpack 120
LINUXspeak.. 120
Sample 121
Dissecting E-Mail Addresses 121
Managing E-Mail with elm 122
Creating mail aliases 122

Exiting elm 123
Getting help 124
Printing a message... 124
Reading a message 124
Reading other mail files 125
Saving a message 125
Sending a message... 126
Tagging messages 126
Using elm options 127
Managing E-Mail with pine 127
Exiting pine 127
Printing a message... 128
Reading a message 128
Saving a message 128
Sending a message 128
Working with attachments 129
Using fetchmail for Remote Mail Access 129
LINUXspeak.. 130

Part VII: Working with the Other Guys 131

Working with MS-DOS Media.. 132
Mtools Basics 132
mcd — Changing the current directory 133
mcopy — Copying files between DOS disks 133
mdel — Deleting MS-DOS files 134
mdir — Displaying an MS-DOS directory 134
minfo — Printing MS-DOS file system parameters 134
mmd — Making a new directory 135
mtype — Displaying file contents 135
xcopy — Copying one directory to another 135
More Mtools commands 136
Mounting MS-DOS Media and Partitions 136
Mounting hard disk partitions 136
Mounting and unmounting removable media 137
Working with Mac Media 137
hcd — Changing the hfs working directory 138
hcopy — Copying files to or from an hfs volume 138
hdel — Deleting files from an HFS volume 138
hdir — Listing the files in an HFS directory................. 139
hmkdir — Creating a new directory.............................. 139
hmount — Mounting an HFS volume 139
humount — Unmounting an HFS volume 140
Other hfsutils commands 140
Working with UNIX Files and Media 140

Part VIII: Networking *141*

Deciphering Network Addressing 142
    Domain addresses 142
    IP addresses 142
    Nameservers 142
ftp — Transferring Files 143
    LINUXspeak 143
    Connecting to anonymous FTP servers 143
    Connecting to the remote system 144
    Configuring .netrc for automatic logins 144
    Downloading files with ftp 145
    Executing local commands while in ftp 146
    Exiting ftp 146
    ftp command summary 146
    Listing directory contents with ftp 147
    Navigating the remote host with ftp 147
    Transferring multiple files with ftp 148
    Uploading files with ftp 148
nslookup — Querying Internet Name Servers 148
ping — Sending Test Packets to Network Hosts 150
rcp — Copying Remote Files 151
rlogin — Logging in Remotely................................... 152
    Connecting to the remote host using rlogin 153
    Terminating your rlogin session 153
rsh — Executing Commands Remotely 153
Setting Up Your System to Use rlogin and rsh without
   Passwords 155
    Using /etc/hosts.equiv 155
    Using .rhosts 155
telnet — Logging in Remotely.................................. 156
    LINUXspeak 156
    Connecting to the remote host using telnet 156
    Sample 157
    Terminating your telnet session 157
traceroute — Finding the Route to a Remote Host 157
whois — Accessing DNS Registration Information 159

Part IX: Systems Administration *163*

Adding Users 164
Checking File Systems 165
Deleting Users 165
Finding System Files 166
Managing User Control Files 167
    The group file 167
    The password file 167

Shadow passwords 168
Networking with PPP 168
The chat program 170
LINUXspeak 170
Fixing the routing 172
Mail servers 173
Making the connection 174
Name servers 174
The News server 174
Phone number and login sequence 175
The pppd program 175
Setting Up Serial Ports for User Login 178
Shutting Down LINUX 179
Starting LINUX 180
Using the cron Program 180
Working with Run Levels 180
Adding a new start or kill file 181
Changing run levels 181
Example inittab file 182
Setting up files in the run level directories 183
System run levels 184

Part X: Using Regular Expressions 187
Examining Simple Regular Expressions 188
Combining Simple Regular Expressions 188
Samples of Basic Regular Expressions 189

Online Resources 191
General Web Resources 192
Distribution Web Pages 192
FTP Resources 192
Magazines 193
Usenet Newsgroups 193

Techie Talk 195
Index 201

How to Use This Book

LINUX For Dummies Quick Reference fills you in on some of the basic capabilities of the LINUX system, along with an assortment of those that aren't so widely used — commands and options you would discover only after years of experience using LINUX.

Although this book isn't the whole story on LINUX, I have tried to provide you with the most amount of useful information possible in a compact reference. For instance, descriptions of LINUX commands include examples of their usage to illustrate how LINUX syntax really works.

To find what you need, you can either browse through the book and scan the section headings for relevant entries (most of which are alphabetized), or turn to the Table of Contents or the Index for more help in locating information on using LINUX.

How This Book Is Organized

LINUX For Dummies Quick Reference contains 11 parts and a glossary of terms to help you find things fast.

Part I, "Getting to Know LINUX," starts with the story of how LINUX came to be. It then provides advice for selecting the LINUX distribution that is right for you, LINUX installation information, and tips for dealing with any problems you may encounter during the installation process.

Part II, "Understanding the Shell," introduces the available shells (the command interpreters) and examines the file structure of LINUX. I discuss the basic capabilities of the shell, concentrating on Bash. Don't miss the table of characters that have special meaning to the shell.

Part III, "Common Shell Commands," is where the most commonly used LINUX commands can be found. I divide the commands into functional groups — such as Sorting, Searching, or Printing — alphabetically within the groups.

Part IV, "Using X/FVWM," covers the X Window System and FVWM, the most common window manager. It includes keyboard short-cuts for working with X and information on how to work with nongraphical programs in this graphical environment.

Part V, "Text Editors and Working with Text," offers information on how to use two text editors — pico and joe — that are designed for beginners, and how to use two powerhouse text editors — Emacs and vi. This part also covers spell-checking and text formatting.

Part VI, "Sending and Receiving E-Mail," explains how electronic mail works in LINUX. It covers Pine and elm, the two most common mail user agents, and tells you how to get your e-mail from your Internet service provider.

Part VII, "Working with the Other Guys," shows you how to handle files from the MS-DOS/Windows, Macintosh, and UNIX environments.

Part VIII, "Networking," describes the tools you need to test network connectivity, transfer files over a network, and work interactively on remote computers.

Part IX, "Systems Administration," takes you beyond the scope of the individual user and into the realm of system administration. You can read about routine systems work, such as adding users and checking files systems, or more advance operations such as establishing a PPP (Point-to-Point Protocol) connection to your ISP.

Part X, "Using Regular Expressions," is a concise reference on regular expressions, which are used by many LINUX editors and other programs for searching and matching text patterns.

The appendix, "Online Resources," offers a list of places to search for software, user groups, documentation, and lots more information on LINUX.

The glossary of terms, "Techie Talk," contains an alphabetical listing of technical terms used in this book and in the LINUX community. Go to the glossary when you need an unfamiliar term translated into English.

Conventions Used in This Book

When I include LINUX commands and lines of code, they are presented `in this typeface`. For example:

`cp *.food ~/Html/`

When you're instructed to type something exactly as it appears in the text, it is presented in `boldface`. For example: Type **man at**.

In the "LINUXspeak" sections, *italics* are used to indicate that they are to be replaced with the actual name you are using, usually the name of a file. Square brackets are used to indicate optional information that is not part of the command itself. How you should use the information in the brackets is explained in the Options or Arguments table that follows the commands themselves. For example:

`cat [-E] [-n] [-T] [-v]` *files*

(By the way, the conventions used in the book are also common to much of the LINUX online documentation, such as the man pages.)

Need More Information?

No book this size can provide every user with every answer to every question. While I don't have the space to list all the options for every command, I can give you the most common and most important ones you're likely to need.

If you are looking for more detailed information about a particular command, use the `man` command (***see*** Part III for more on `man`). `man` is the built-in LINUX command that prints techno-help documentation. Or, check out the Appendix, "Online Resources" for other sources of information.

Icons Used in This Book

Throughout out this book you'll find icons that point out information that may prove to be especially useful.

 These are helpful hints that can save you some keystrokes or be used to impress your coworkers.

 This icon flags mistakes I've made myself at one time. I learned from those mistakes and am now passing that wisdom on to you.

 This icon appears next to a command or feature that doesn't work the way you would expect.

 This icon alerts you to system administration commands that can be executed only by the super user (a.k.a, root).

## Part 1

Getting to Know LINUX

The capabilities of the LINUX operating system rival that of commercial products that cost big companies millions of dollars to develop, but with one big difference — LINUX is available free to anyone who wants it. As you find out more about LINUX you can see what made it possible in the first place as well as what it can accomplish for you.

For you UNIX users out there, LINUX offers all the familiar UNIX capabilities and features, plus a few new capabilities that you may have wished for on your UNIX system.

In this part . . .

✔ **Understanding the origin of LINUX**

✔ **Finding out about LINUX distributions**

✔ **Installing LINUX**

What Is LINUX?

LINUX is a multiuser, multitasking operating system that runs on PCs, as well as many other computers. It implements a superset of the POSIX (IEEE P1003.*x*) operating system standard that was created in order to document a standard set of UNIX capabilities. LINUX includes all these capabilities plus it draws on the best capabilities of BSD UNIX and System V UNIX to offer a well-rounded and capable operating system. LINUX also interoperates with other systems, including Microsoft Windows, MacOS, UNIX, and Novell.

LINUX was the brainchild of a college student named Linus Torvalds. In 1990, while a computer science student at the University of Helsinki in Finland, Torvalds decided that writing a UNIX-like operating system would be interesting. Over the following years, LINUX grew from one person's idea into a personal experiment and worldwide effort by thousands of people around the world to write a UNIX clone.

Today, millions of people use LINUX. Some individuals are using it as a way to learn about operating systems. However, many businesses also depend on LINUX for a number of applications. LINUX is currently being used on desktops at companies as large and as well-known as Hewlett-Packard, in embedded systems such as Point of Sale from Schlumberger, and by Internet Service Providers worldwide.

Some of LINUX's strengths include the following:

+ **Adaptability:** The source code for LINUX is freely available to anyone. This means that you can make modifications to the code to add other capabilities or enable LINUX to work with unique hardware.

+ **Interoperability:** LINUX-based systems can be connected to most other computer platforms.

+ **Price:** LINUX is available free of charge and is licensed under the GNU General Public License (GPL), which allows and encourages users to share code with others.

LINUX has the look, feel, and smell of a UNIX system. What distinguishes LINUX from a commercial version of UNIX is that it is not a product of a company or of an individual, but rather a cooperative effort on the part of developers and users worldwide to produce something that meets their own computing requirements.

Unlike most commercial software development, LINUX has no "marketing department" dictating what it thinks users need. Development follows the path set by Torvalds (considered a minor deity in many developer circles) and his "kernel-hacking cabal." The introduction of new features into LINUX is spontaneous and dynamic, and is dominated by a casual mob rule among techno-geeks on the Internet.

Selecting a LINUX Flavor

Much like UNIX versions and very unlike Microsoft operating systems, multiple flavors (formally known as *distributions*) of LINUX are available. These flavors, (or versions or distributions, whichever you prefer), come from various companies and organizations.

To make a distribution, a vendor takes the basic LINUX operating system and utility programs and adds value to the system and programs. This added value is generally a combination of the vendor's installation method, some proprietary programs, and technical support.

The difference between the distributions is in many ways like the difference between a Ford and a Chevy — they pretty much work the same, just with a different "nameplate" and a few different features. The most popular distributions today are the following:

- ✦ **Caldera:** A series of proprietary distributions that include LINUX and additional licensed software from Caldera Corporation. Information on Caldera is available at www.caldera.com. (**Note:** The whole distribution is not available on the Web site — just some information and a few of the parts.)

- ✦ **Debian:** A completely free distribution put together by a set of volunteers. Information on Debian is available at www.debian.org.

- ✦ **Red Hat:** A very popular commercial distribution that is also available for free. Information on Red Hat is available at www.redhat.com.

- ✦ **Slackware:** Another commercial distribution, which is also available for free. Information on Slackware is available at www.cdrom.com.

Most of these distributions, minus the technical support, are available for free (according to the LINUX general public license). The exact same versions of Red Hat and Slackware that you can buy are also available for free.

No single distribution is right for everyone. Among various LINUX distributions, differences exist in cost, included capabilities such as installation methods and add-on programs, supported platforms, and user support. For example, some versions of Caldera include the Netscape web browser and the StarOffice office suite. If you need these products, purchasing Caldera is probably the right choice. On the other hand, if you want to be a part of the cooperative evolution of LINUX itself, Debian may be the best choice.

In any case, all of the products are based on the same LINUX kernel and programs. Because of the general public license, programmers who make innovations or improvements to the LINUX source code must make those changes available to all LINUX users.

Some vendors produce LINUX *archive CDs,* which contain an assortment of LINUX software from various sites on the Internet. A typical archive set may contain the Debian, Red Hat, and Slackware distributions, along with other LINUX software. Archive CDs usually sell for around $25. The following are the two most popular archive CD packages:

+ **InfoMagic** at www.infomagic.com

+ **Pacific HighTech** at www.pht.com

Besides purchasing a LINUX distribution on CD, many ftp sites on the Internet have copies available for download. Two popular examples are:

+ sunsite.unc.edu — Sunsite offers http as well as ftp access to the LINUX Documentation Project pages at sunsite.unc.edu/LDP, and is mirrored at many other sites, including www.infomagic.com.

+ tsx-11.mit.edu — ftp access only. This site typically contains more of the cutting-edge development releases of software than does Sunsite.

If you elect to download LINUX over the Internet, find a site that has the distribution you are interested in and follow the download directions. For example, to download Debian, point your web browser at www.debian.org. From that page, you can find a download location near you and go for it.

On the practical side of things, however, you are generally better off to get a LINUX CD. The CDs are inexpensive and the sheer volume of LINUX software makes downloading a serious time commitment.

Another place to look for generic information on LINUX is SSC's LINUX resources page at www.ssc.com/LINUX. From there you can find links to LINUX International, LINUX User Groups, the LINUX Speaker's Bureau, *LINUX Gazette* (an e-zine), and *LINUX Journal* — a monthly magazine about LINUX.

Installing LINUX

All the distributions discussed in the preceding section are available on CD. Debian and Red Hat also support installation over the Internet. While some installation differences exist among each flavor of LINUX, the following list shows the basic steps that you must perform to install any version:

1. Make some space available for LINUX on your hard drive. You can do so by adding an additional hard drive to your computer or by repartitioning your current hard drive.

If you elect to repartition your hard drive, you can use a program called FIPS (First Interactive Partitioning System), which is available on most distribution CDs and at archive sites. FIPS shows the amount of free space on your MS-DOS partitions and allows you to reduce the size of the existing partitions to free up some space. I have found FIPS totally reliable, but, before you start repartitioning, you should do a full backup of your hard drive, just to be safe.

The amount of space that you need depends on how much of LINUX you want to load and what you intend to do with it. The LINUX kernel and a basic set of utilities could easily fit on a disk partition as small as 50MB. When you start loading pieces such as the language compilers and GUI interface, the required disk space grows significantly. On the other end of the spectrum, loading every part of LINUX can take more than 500MB.

2. Once you have a place for LINUX, you need to load it and start the installation process. The most common way to boot LINUX is from a floppy disk set. If you purchase a distribution directly from Red Hat, it includes a boot disk. You can mount the CD on any system supporting standard ISO-9660 file systems and write the necessary disks. If you are doing this from an MS-DOS system, you can use the rawrite.exe program included on the CD.

If your computer has a bootable CD-ROM drive, you may be able to boot LINUX directly from the CD. The Debian (since Version 1.3) distribution allows you to do this.

3. Once you boot the LINUX installation program, it interacts with you to guide you through the installation process. Each distribution is different, but the basic process remains the same. The installation process includes the repartitioning of your hard drive (even if you did it earlier, you still need to set the partition types to LINUX), the formatting of the partition or partitions, selection of the packages to load, and the actual loading process.

4. Somewhere along the way, the installation program asks if you want to run the X Window System (more commonly called *X*). X is the graphical user interface common to all LINUX and UNIX systems. X isn't required to use LINUX and it does use a lot of disk space. You may want to initially load LINUX without X.

5. At the tail end of the installation process, the installation program asks you if you want to install LILO (the LINUX LOader). LILO allows you to select which operating system to start each time you reboot your computer. You can safely install LILO on the master boot record of your primary hard drive. In the installation process, all you have to do is tell LILO about other operating systems you want it to boot.

6. Finally, you should always make a *rescue disk*. This is a boot disk for your particular system. If something happens and you cannot boot off the hard drive, you can boot off the rescue disk, mount the LINUX partition from your hard drive, and look for the problem.

Fixing Installation Problems

Nothing is completely foolproof. This is my way of saying that problems can occur during installation of LINUX. Here are a few of the most common ones and their possible causes.

Errors while booting from a floppy

The most common causes of this problem are that either the floppy disk itself is bad or you downloaded a bad file. Try writing to a new floppy, and, if you downloaded the *boot image* over the Internet, try downloading it again. (All distributions have boot disk images on their CDs, which are copies of what is on the CD.)

If you bought a copy of LINUX that included a boot floppy and a CD, a boot image should appear on the CD. Locate this image, copy it to a new floppy, and try booting again.

System gets hung up during the boot

First, remember that booting from a floppy can take some time. If the floppy drive light is on, the boot process is probably in the works. But, you should keep a couple of things in minds:

✦ The first step in booting from a floppy is to load LILO. Each letter of the word LILO is displayed for each step in the boot process. If only some of the letters display (*L* and *I,* for example), this may indicate that some sort of error has occurred. Refer to the LILO documentation on the LINUX CD to determine the exact problem.

✦ During the boot process, routines in the various device drivers probe the hardware to determine addresses and interrupts. It is possible that a routine probing for one device (an Ethernet card, for example) may instead probe for a different device (such as a sound or SCSI card), which causes the system to hang. One way to try to isolate this problem is to remove all nonessential cards from the computer and try the boot again. If this works, add the cards one at a time until the problem crops up again.

System says it's out of memory

Most installation programs use what's called a *RAMdisk,* which means that a portion of the RAM in the computer is allocated to act as a file system. Make sure you are allocating and activating swap space during the installation. (*Swap space* is allocated space on the hard drive that LINUX can use as an extension of RAM. During the installation process, answer Yes to both messages you get about swap space allocation and activation.)

You get a "Cylinder > 1023" error message

LINUX doesn't use your computer's BIOS (basic input/output system) after it is booted, but it does use BIOS in the boot process. Because of a BIOS limitation, all of the partition you intend to boot must fall below cylinder 1024. This may require your moving some partitions around or installing a small boot partition and then placing most of LINUX on another partition.

You get an "Unable to Mount" message

This means that the system is unable to mount the LINUX root directory or unable to mount the CD. Make sure the CD is inserted completely in the drive and that the CD is recognized (you'll know if the CD is recognized by the boot messages telling you the CD-ROM drive was found at a particular address).

Win95 made LINUX vanish

If you install Windows 95 after you install LINUX, Win 95 will wipe out LILO. The solution is to either boot LINUX from a floppy or to reinstall LILO after you install Windows 95.

You're having hardware problems

LINUX now runs on most hardware (although you may find some older SCSI disk controllers or Ethernet cards that aren't supported).

✦ If get an "unable to access the CD or disk drive" message, read the boot messages. If you don't see a message about a device that you know exists among your hardware, you probably have a device that is unsupported by LINUX.

✦ Many users receive memory errors when running LINUX on a system that ran MS-DOS with no problems. These errors usually indicate something's wrong with your hardware. Because LINUX takes advantage of more system features (such as overlapping DMA I/O transfers while using the CPU for other tasks), a less-than-totally-reliable memory chip or faulty motherboard can cause these problems.

✦ To diagnose a problem, first remove any unnecessary hardware, such as an Ethernet card. If the problem goes away, hardware may be the culprit or there may be a conflict in an address or IRQ (Interrupt Request).

## Part II

Understanding the Shell

The shell is the *command interpreter* — it acts as your interface to the operating system by accepting your input and performing the tasks you request.

Before I get into the nitty-gritty of shells, let me mention that graphical user interfaces are available for LINUX. That means for those of you who prefer the point-and-grunt interface of a mouse, there is hope.

In this part . . .

- ✔ Picking the shell that's best for you

- ✔ Getting programs to read and write files

- ✔ Connecting the output of one program to the input of another program

- ✔ Using quotes to control the interpretation of your input

- ✔ Customizing your environment

- ✔ Getting familiar with shell conventions

- ✔ Examining special characters and what they do

Available Shells

Multiple shells are included with LINUX distributions. They include ash, Bash, ksh, tcsh, and zsh. The most popular shell by far is Bash, a product of the GNU Project of the Free Software Foundation. Bash stands for *Bourne Again SHell* (named after Stephen Bourne, who wrote the first programmable shell for UNIX).

In this book, I use the Bash shell as the standard. As a user, you may want to consider ksh as an alternative — particularly if you work with UNIX platforms. The ksh shell is a public-domain implementation of the POSIX-compliant Korn shell, which was written by David Korn at AT&T. The ksh shell is commonly available on most UNIX platforms.

Basic Directory Commands

Use the following commands to perform basic directory management tasks.

cd dirname — To change your current directory

mkdir dirnames — To create a new directory

rmdir *dirname* — To remove an empty directory

pwd — To find out which directory you're in

Type pwd (for print working directory) and the name of the current directory appears on screen. To verify the name of your home directory, type pwd after logging in.

Character Quoting

Some characters have a special meaning to the shell (that is, the shell treats the characters as directions to perform some action). If you need to enter these characters as part of a filename, and you don't want the shell to interpret their special meaning, then you need to *quote* these characters.

Quoting an individual character

To quote any single character, precede it with a backslash (\). For example, to list the names of all files that contain an *, type this:

ls -a ***

In the previous line of code, the shell interprets the first and third asterisk but not the second one. Therefore, it matches any set of characters that contains an asterisk.

You can use double and single quotes (" and ') to quote whole strings. Their meaning is somewhat different.

✦ Single quotes quote almost everything.

✦ Double quotes allow the shell to interpret words that start with a $, which are commonly known as *shell variable references.*

✦ You can use a single quote to turn off the special meaning of a double quote and vice versa.

For example, in the following command, the double quotes prevent the shell from interpreting the special meaning of the single quote in it's but they allow $money to be treated as a reference to a shell variable. The double quotes also prevent the shell from interpreting the white space so that it's my $money is treated as a single argument rather than three separate ones.

```
grep "it's my $money" junkfile
```

Using the close-quote character

The single close-quote character (') is useful for telling the shell to execute a command within the back quotes, insert the output of the execution into the original command line in place of the command in back quotes, and then execute the newly built command line. You can use this trick to display a message that contains the current date.

```
echo Gee, today is 'date' soon it will be my
    birthday
```

Command History

The Bash shell maintains a command history, a list of up to 500 of the most recently entered commands. If you type the command history, the shell displays your history list.

The history command is useful when you want to reexecute a command without having to retype it. (The number of commands saved can be changed by setting the HISTSIZE shell variable.) You can then use the commands described in the following sections to go back through the list and edit and reexecute a command.

Setting command history mode

How you edit recent commands depends on whether your shell is set to vi mode or Emacs mode.

✦ For vi mode, type set -o vi and press Enter.

✦ For Emacs mode, type set -o emacs and press Enter.

Using Emacs mode

If you are in Emacs mode, you can press Ctrl+P to access the previous command, press Ctrl+N to access the next command, or use the arrow keys. When you finish editing, press Enter to execute the command. (*See* Part V for details on the available editing commands.)

Using vi mode

If you are in vi mode, press Esc and then use standard vi commands (k to move up, j to move down, and so on) to access and edit the history list. When you are ready to execute the edited command, press Enter. (*See* Part V for details on the available editing commands.)

Customizing the Environment

LINUX, in the UNIX tradition, has always allowed you to customize your work environment, and this section shows you some of the ways to do that.

Creating shell aliases

While you can use shell and environment variables to remember what's in a character string, a shell alias is specifically designed to allow you to make up names for commands.

LINUXspeak

alias [*name*[=*command*]]

Argument	Function
name	The name of the alias. If not specified, alias lists all your current aliases.
command	Command string assigned to the alias. If *command* contains any spaces or special characters, it must be quoted.

Sample

Suppose that you want to occasionally print files on a printer named soy (instead of on your default printer). Normally you type lpr -P soy *file* to print to the other printer, but you want an easier way. The following command establishes an alias called lpsoy that would do this for you.

```
alias lpsoy='lpr -P soy'
```

Once the alias is created, you can direct your printer output to printer soy by using the alias. For example, to print the file lentil.loaf, type lpsoy lentil.loaf.

You can used the unalias command to delete a shell alias. For example, to delete your alias lpsoy, type unalias lpsoy.

Displaying environment variables

Any environment variable is also available as a shell variable, so you can display an environment variable just as you would a shell variable — by using the $ prefix as an argument to a command (such as echo) that displays the value of its arguments.

LINUXspeak
echo $var

Option or Argument	Function
var	Name of the environment (or shell) variable to display

Figuring out which variables are local to your current shell and which are from the environment can be confusing. Type export with no variable names to see a list of variables that are exported.

Sample

Suppose that you have written some shell scripts that e-mail recipes to your fellow vegetarians. The scripts need to know where you keep your list of e-mail addresses. The shell scripts also need to know the name of the directory where the recipes are located. The easiest way to pass this information would be to set some environment variables. Whenever the shell starts the scripts, the scripts can just read in the values.

```
export veg_ADDRESSES=~/Addr/veggie
export RECIPES=~/Recipes/Veg
```

Setting environment variables

Environment variables are saved in such a way that they are available to any shell that is a child of the current shell. Thus, environment variables are the right place to save things like your search path and the name of your printer.

LINUXspeak
export var=value

or

var=value
export var

The order of the commands doesn't matter in the preceding example. The `export` statement performs the binding. If the shell variable is already set, its current value is exported to the environment. If the value is changed at a later time, the environment variable follows the value of the shell variable.

Option or Argument	Function
var	Name of the variable to set
value	A string value to be assigned. You must quote *value* if it contains spaces or other characters that have special meaning to the shell.

If you want to invoke one command with a different value for either a shell or environment variable, but not change its value subsequent to the command, you can specify the variable value on the command line. For example, to run a script called `way_cool` with the `PRINTER` variable set to `fastone`, just type `PRINTER=fastone way_cool`.

Setting shell editing modes

With the Bash and Korn shells, you have your choice whether to use vi-style or Emacs-style command line editing (*see* Part V). My advice is that if you use the vi or Emacs text editor, set your shell mode to the editing mode that matches your editor (which will help you get more comfortable with your editor). If you don't currently use either editor, try each mode and pick the one that you are most comfortable with.

To set the shell mode to vi, use the following command:

```
set -o vi
```

To set the shell mode to Emacs, use this command:

```
set -o emacs
```

You can place either of these commands in your .profile file so that the mode will be automatically set at login time.

One significant difference between the using the editing commands in vi and those in Emacs is that in vi mode you need to press Esc to activate the editing command (you have to switch back and forth between insert and command mode in vi command-line mode). In Emacs, you need to just type the key combinations as shown in the following table.

Emacs	vi	Function
Ctrl+P	K	Moves back one command in your history list
Ctrl+N	J	Moves forward one line in your history list
Ctrl+B	H	Moves back one character in the displayed command line
Ctrl+F	L	Moves forward one character in the displayed command line
Esc+B	b	Moves backward one word
Esc+F	f	Moves forward one word
Ctrl+A	0	Moves to beginning of line
Ctrl+E	$	Moves to end of line
	i	Enter insert mode
	Esc	Exit insert mode
	a	Appends to line
Esc+Del	X	Deletes backward one character
Ctrl+D	x	Deletes forward one character
Esc+D	dw	Delete forward one word
Esc+K	D	Deletes forward to end of line
Esc+.	Esc+_	Inserts last word of previous command

After you've mastered these commands, check out the man pages (enter man bash or man ksh) for additional editing commands.

Standard environment variables

Environment variables are used to set your working environment. You change their values to change your default environment. You may also want to add new variables that your own programs use.

Variable	Function
DISPLAY	Display location (for the X Window System)
HOME	Path to your home directory
HOSTNAME	Name of this computer system
LOGNAME	Your login name
MAIL	Path to your e-mail file
PATH	Command search path — colon-separated list. For example, PATH may have the value /bin:/usr/bin:/usr/local/bin/~/bin
SHELL	Path to default shell
TERM	Terminal type

Sample

Say that you want to create a new environment variable called WOW and set it to be equal to the directory path where you keep all your good files. Then you can reference this directory any time you want to copy or access a file in that directory.

The following commands set the variable and then list the file super from that directory using the less command. Placing the export command in your .profile file makes WOW available every time you log on.

```
export WOW=/home/tofu/Good-files
less $WOW/stew.txt
```

To add a new directory to your current search path, enter PATH=$PATH:*newdir*.

This command adds a new directory named *newdir* to the end of the path (last directory to be searched).

Directory Naming Conventions

A popular practice is to name directories with a leading capital letter (for example, Correspondence or Secret). This way, all directories display together in a file list (ls) and are easily identified. (*See* Part III for details.)

If you are unsure which entries in a list are directories, type ls -F and press Enter. A / is displayed at the end of any directories.

Directory Referencing

A reliable way to access a file in your home directory (or one of its branches) is to use a tilde (~). It acts as an abbreviation for the path to your home directory For example, if your current directory is not your home directory but you want to get a list of the files in your home directory, you can type ls ~ as an alternative to ls /home/phil.

You can also follow the tilde with a user name (such as ~tempeh) to access information in the directory of the user named *tempeh*. For example, to change your current directory to a directory named Carrots that is in the home of a user whose login name is tempeh, type cd ~tempeh/Carrots.

Files Associated with a Program

Whenever you start a LINUX program, three files are associated
with the program. In LINUXspeak, these files are referred to as:

+ stdin for *standard input*

+ stdout for *standard output*

+ stderr for *standard error*

Redirecting the files

The files associated with a LINUX program are all initially
associated with both your keyboard and display, but you can
also connect the files to other files and programs. The following
table lists characters you can use to redirect the files.

Redirection Character	What It Does
>	Redirects the output of the command to a file or device.
>>	Acts like >, but if the file already exists, this character appends the new data to the end of an existing file. If the file does not exist, it is created.
2>	Redirects the error output (also called stderr) of the command to a file or device. (Error output is a second output file available to every program. The program itself decides which output to write to stdout and which to write to stderr.)
<	Redirects the input of the command from a file or device.
|	Joins two simple commands so they work together in a more useful way. (This character is called a *pipe*. *See* the next section "Connecting commands" for more on pipes.)

Connecting commands

Many commands can read from standard input and write to standard
output. LINUX calls commands that can do this *filters*. The name
comes from the fact that they are filtering whatever comes in to
produce whatever is supposed to come out.

Filters allow commands to connect to other commands through *pipes*
or to become part of a *pipeline.* When using the pipe character (|)
with two commands, the pipe connects the output of the left-hand
command to the input of the right-hand command. For example,
ls -la | less pipes the output of the file list command (ls)
into the input of the less command, which allows you to scroll
back and forth through the file listing.

System resources present the only limitation on how many commands can be connected together in this way. For example, the `grep` command is a filter. It can read standard input, apply some selection criteria to the input, and then send the selected information to standard output. The following pipeline can run the program `monthly`, filter its output through `grep` (in this case, looking for lines with the word `super` in them), and display the selected lines on the screen.

```
monthly | grep super
```

Redirecting command output

The `>` operator is used to redirect the output of a command to a file or device. For example, to cause the output of the program `monthly` to be redirected to a new file called monthly.output, you would enter the command

```
monthly > monthly.output
```

If you want to append to an existing file, use the `>>` operator. Working with this example, if you want to append to an existing file called monthly.output instead of creating a new file, use

```
monthly >> monthly.output
```

If `monthly.output` does not exist, `>>` acts just like `>` and creates a new file.

The filename /dev/tty is a special name that always points at your screen. If you write a shell script in which you want the output of one command to come back to the screen no matter where stdout and stderr are redirected, redirect that command's output to /dev/tty.

Redirecting command input

To indicate that the input for a command is to come from a file rather than your keyboard, you use the `<` operator. For example, to run a program named monthly and have it read from the file input.data, use

```
monthly < input.data
```

You can combine input redirection with other redirection. To run monthly with its input coming from input.data, its output sent to monthly.output, and its error output coming back to the screen (a pretty typical situation), use

```
monthly < input.data > monthly.output
```

Redirecting error messages

If you want to redirect the error messages from a program to a file, use the 2> operator. For example, if you want the error messages from program monthly to be sent to monthly.errors, use

```
monthly 2> monthly.errors
```

You can redirect both stderr and stdout to different places. For example, to append the standard output of monthly to monthly.output and send the error messages to monthly.errors, use

```
monthly >> monthly.output 2> monthly.errors
```

If you want to run a command and redirect both stdout and stderr, you need to use the command 2>&1 which means essentially, "redirect output stream 2 to the same place as output stream 1." For example, to redirect the stdout and stderr of monthly to monthly.both you would use

```
monthly >monthly.both 2>&1
```

File Naming Conventions

LINUX does not impose any structure on the name of a file — other than you cannot use a slash character (/) in a filename, and the length of the filename must be less than 256 characters. While this state of anarchy may sound desirable to some, you should follow certain file-naming conventions to keep yourself out of trouble. When in doubt, keep filenames simple.

In LINUX, filenames are case-sensitive. The file carrot is different from Carrot, CARROT, or cArRoT. These three files may all live happily together in the same directory.

Some special characters, which are technically legal to use in a filename, may get you into trouble because of their other meanings. The following table offers better-safe-than-sorry choices for filenames characters.

Lower-case letters	Always safe to use.
Upper-case letters	Always safe to use, but many people reserve them for directory names.
Numbers	Always safe to use.
Underscores (_)	Always safe to use — they make good word separators.
Hyphens	Don't use as a first character.
Commas	Always safe to use.
Periods	Always safe to use.

See the section "Special Characters," later in this part, for an explanation of the meaning other characters have to the shell.

Pathnames

A file's *pathname* consists of the file's full name, starting at the root of the file tree. Therefore, if your home directory is /home/ tofu, and you have a subdirectory called Secret, and within that directory you have a file called love.letters, the pathname of love.letters would be /home/tofu/Secret/love.letters. This file is totally distinct from a file with a similar name in a different directory such as /home/tempeh/Secret/love.letters or /home/ tofu/Correspondence/love.letters.

Shell Command Elements

When you want to instruct the shell to perform a task, you need to pass it a whole set of information. The basic elements of a shell command are the following:

+ The name of the command to run

+ Any command line options that you want to use

+ Any arguments required by the command

+ Intructions on how to handle the input and output data streams

For instance, here's an example of a shell command:

```
diff -i first second > result
```

+ `diff`, the first word on the line is the name of the command you are asking the shell to run.

+ `-i` is an option (the hyphen is a tip-off). Options must generally appear between the command name and the arguments.

+ `first` is the first argument.

+ `second` is the second argument.

+ `>` is a redirection operator. It redirects the output of the command to a file. (*See* the section "Files Associated with a Program" earlier in this part.)

+ `result` is the name of the file where the command output is redirected.

+ Each of these items is commonly called a *word*. The words of the shell command are separated by *whitespace,* which is defined as one or more space or tab characters.

The most basic command consists of only a command name. For example, to display the current date, type date and press Enter.

Most shells interpret the redirection operator first, and then parse the other command parameters. For that reason, a line consisting only of output redirection and a filename (for example, >peach_cobbler) creates an empty file called peach_cobbler. (***See also*** the section "Files Associated with a Program," earlier in this part, for an understanding of the redirection operator.)

Some commands need *arguments* to operate. For example, if you want to edit a text file with vi (which I like to call "the world's greatest editor"), you need to tell the editor the name of the file. Thus, vi myfile starts up the editor and tells it to open a file named myfile. (***See*** Part V for more on vi.)

The third type of information that is passed to a command is a *command line option*. Options modify the operation of a command. For example, ls lists the files in your current directory, but it does not display files with names beginning with a dot. (These are known as hidden files.) The -a option (ls -a) instructs ls to include in the output those that have files names starting with a dot.

Shell Variables

Shell variables are a local place for your shell to store information. For example, the shell variable HOME is set to the pathname of your login directory. In Bash and ksh, you can set shell variables to *environment variables* by the use of the export statement.

The difference between shell variables and environment variables is that variables are available to the shells that you start up later. Shell variables, on the other hand, are used only in the shell in which they were created. Shell variables are identified by placing a $ (dollar sign) in front of the variable name.

The following sequence sets the shell variable DOG to the value Beagle. The second line exports the shell variable to an environment variable. The third line then displays the environment variable using the echo command.

```
DOG=Beagle
export DOG
echo My dog is a $DOG
```

✦ If your login shell is Bash, zsh, or ksh, then the environment variables in ~/.profile are used every time you log in.

✦ The .bashrc file contains environment variables that are used as the default settings for the Bash shell.

✦ The equivalent files for csh and tcsh are .login and .cshrc.

The following table shows the standard shell variables:

Shell Variable	What It Means
$?	Return status of last command (0 indicates success — whatever the command considers a successful execution)
HOME	Pathname of your home directory
MAIL	Name of the file to check for incoming mail
OLDPWD	Pathname of current directory before previous cd command
PWD	Your current directory
SHELL	Pathname of your shell

Many common shell variables are available. Type set to see your current variables and their assigned values.

Special Characters

Many characters have special meanings to the shell. The characters and their meanings vary from shell to shell and system to system. Use the documentation on your shell and the stty command to verify these characters. The following list offers code examples showing the proper way to use the stty command. The table that follows the list provides likely default meanings for some keyboard entries and characters.

✦ To display all your current terminal settings, type stty -a.

✦ To change a stty mode that is either true or false, type stty followed by the name of the mode to turn it on. To turn a mode off, precede the name with a -. For example, to turn off the opost mode, type stty -opost.

✦ To change the value of a setting, type stty *name value*. For example, to change the erase command to Control+H, you would type stty erase, then press Ctrl+H.

Special Entry	What It Does
Enter	Tells the shell that your command is ready to be processed.
Spacebar or Tab	Separates words in commands. In Bash, Tab prompts the shell to complete the current word into a match with a filename, login name (if it starts with ~), hostname (if it starts with @), or shell variable (if it starts with a $).

Special Entry	*What It Does*
Backspace or Delete	Either key deletes the most recently typed character. Use stty to change the backspace character.
;	Command separator. Allows you to enter multiple commands on the same line.
&	When placed at the end of a command line, this character starts the command in the line preceding the & in the background and returns a shell prompt immediately. You can use && between commands to represent a logical AND. The second command executes only if the first command completes successfully.
|	Connects the standard output of the command on the left to the standard input of the command on the right. || can be used between commands to mean a logical OR. The second command executes only if the first one fails.
!	In Bash and tcsh, this character denotes a history reference. When this character is followed by the beginning of a command, the history list is searched backward for the most recent command that matches.
#	Comment. The remainder of the line is ignored by the shell.
\	Takes away the special meaning of a special character that follows it. Can escape the Enter character allowing you to continue commands onto a subsequent line.
'	Disables the special meaning of characters enclosed in single quotes.
"	Disables the special meaning of characters (except for $) enclosed in double quotes.
`	Executes what's in the quoted string and replaces the command in quotes with its output.
$	Introduces a reference to a shell variable.
*	Matches any number of characters.
?	Matches a single character.
[ ]	Matches any single character contained within the braces. For example, [Cat] matches an uppercase C, a lowercase a, or a lowercase t.
Ctrl+C	Sends an interrupt signal to a running program. Use stty to set this character.
Ctrl+D	Sends an end of file to the program currently reading from the keyboard. If you enter Ctrl+D at the shell prompt, it may be interpreted as an end of file to the shell and log you out.
Ctrl+X	Cancels the line you are entering and allows you to start over. Use stty to set this character.
Ctrl+Z	Pauses the current program. You can then use bg to restart the program in the background, fg to restart it in the foreground, or kill to terminate it. You can also type jobs to get a status report of your jobs.

Startup Files

Most startup or configuration files are located in your home directory and have names that start with a dot (.). Bash has two main configuration files:

Startup File	When Bash Reads It
.bash_profile	At login time
.bashrc	Each time a new shell is started

You can force Bash or ksh to read a file and interpret it by using the . (dot) command. For example, you may have some shell variables that you want to set when you are working on a special project. Use your editor to put the commands in a file, name the file .special, and then enter the following command:

. .special

The shell then interprets the file and sets the variables.

The following table shows setup files for both the Bash and Korn shells.

Bash	Korn	Function
/etc/profile	/etc/profile	Executed at login time
$HOME/.profile	$HOME/.profile	Executed at login time
$HOME/.bashrc		Executed at shell startup
$HOME/.bash_logout		Executed at logout

## Part III

Common Shell Commands

Once you know how to talk to the shell, the next thing you need is something to say. In this part, I introduce several dozen LINUX commands (plus examples of how to put them to work) to help you get your jobs done. (You may want to also look at Part II, where I show you how the shell handles commands and how to connect the input and output of your commands.)

In this part . . .

- ✓ Working with files and file content
- ✓ Locating files and content within files
- ✓ Creating and deleting directories
- ✓ Manipulating archives and compressed files

Archiving, Converting, and Other File Manipulation

This section shows you how to work with files within files and with compressed files. If the idea of a file in files sounds strange, consider a file backup, which is the process of copying a bunch of files onto a single place.

cpio — Creating and restoring archive files

Although tar has always been the workhorse of backups, this archiving command has its limitations, such as the length of the pathnames it can handle. As a solution, cpio was introduced in UNIX System V. Today's tar has additional options and cpio can work with different archive formats including tar archives. Criteria for selecting between cpio and tar include:

✦ The cpio format is more portable between different types of computers.

✦ tar is easiest to use to backup a complete file hierarchy.

✦ cpio is much more flexible because it uses an external program or file to specify which files to archive.

✦ tar is available on more computer systems (for example, the suntar program for the Mac) than cpio.

The cpio command has three modes:

✦ **Copy in:** Lists the contents of an archive or restores files from an archive. The -i option specifies copy in mode. Use -it to restrict the operation to a list of the contents.

✦ **Copy out:** Creates an archive. Use -o to specify this mode.

✦ **Pass-thru:** Copies a piece of the file hierarchy from one place to another. Use -p to specify this mode.

LINUXspeak

Copy in: cpio -i [-d] [-F *file*] [-H *fmt*][-m] [-t]
    [-u] [-v] <archive pat

Copy out: cpio -o [-a] [-F *file*] [-H *fmt*] [-v]
    <file_list >archive

Copy-thru: cpio -p [-a] [-d] [-v] <file_list dest_dir

Option or Argument	Function
-a	Restores file access times after copying.
-d	Creates directories as needed.
-F *file*	Uses *file* as archive instead of stdin or stdout.
-H *fmt*	Designates the archive format. You should use newc unless you need to write an archive that's compatible with a system that can't handle the new POSIX standard format. (*See* Part I.)
-m	Retains the modification time of the file when it was archived.
-t	Displays only the archive's table of contents — does not restore any files.
-u	Unconditionally restores the selected files. By default, cpio does overwrite a file that is newer than the one being restored.
-v	Verbose — lists each filename (or file details if used with -t) as the file is being processed.
archive	The file you create in copy out mode or the file you read in copy in mode.
dest_dir	The directory to which cpio copies the selected hierarchy.
file_list	A list of filenames to be selected.
pat	A regular expression-based pattern to select files. Quote this list to prevent interpretation by the shell.

Sample

If you want to back up all the files in the hierarchy under your home directory to a tape (/dev/tape), you can change to your home directory and then use the following commands (note that I first use find to produce the list of filenames):

```
find . -print | cpio -oa >/dev/tape
```

To verify the contents of the tape, use the following command:

```
cpio -itv </dev/tape
```

Now, suppose that you just accidentally deleted all the files whose names end with .favorite from your Vegetables subdirectory. The following command restores those files and preserves their last modify time. Note that I quote the pattern so that the shell does not interpret the *.

```
cpio -imv </dev/tape 'Vegetables/*.favorite'
```

It is very likely that the devices related to backups will not have user read/write permission. If you want to allow users to access these devices, you need to change the permissions (**see** chmod in this part). For example, to allow user read/write of the floppy disk drive, enter the following

```
chmod 666 /dev/fd0
```

gzip — Compressing and decompressing

You can save a lot of disk space by compressing files that you don't access regularly. Furthermore, if you need to occasionally read the compressed files, commands such as zcat allow you to read the file without having to decompress it. The gzip command uses Lempel-Ziv coding, which is nonproprietary. This command is also capable of decompressing files that were compressed with UNIX compress.

LINUXspeak

gzip [-*num*] [-c] [-d] [-r] [-t] [-v] *files*

Option or Argument	Function
-*num*	Level of compression (from 1 to 9). 9 is best but takes longer.
-c	Sends output to stdout. Normally, the input file is deleted and the output file is named the same as the input file, with .gz appended to the filename.
-d	Decompresses instead of compresses.
-r	Recursively compresses or decompresses files within a specified directory.
-t	Tests the integrity of a compressed file.
-v	Verbose — shows how much each file is being compressed.
files	The files to compress or decompress.

Typing gunzip *file* is equivalent to entering gzip -d *file* — and it saves typing two characters.

Sample

Suppose that you have your old recipe files in a directory and you want to compress all of them to save space and you want to see how much space is being saved. Change to the directory that contains your recipe files and enter

```
gzip -v *
```

You can then individually look at the files using zcat; or you can decompress the files by using gunzip.

More compressed file utilities

In addition to zcat, LINUX offers other utilities that work with compressed files. The big difference is that all of these utilities are actually Bourne shell scripts that interpret the command line, invoke gzip to decompress the file, and then pass the result to the regular command. This is the common way to build new tools in the LINUX environment.

Command	Function
zcmp	Decompresses and compares files using cmp
zdiff	Decompresses and compares files using diff
zgrep	Decompresses and searches for patterns using grep
zless	Decompresses and displays file

Sample

Suppose that you have some compressed recipe files and you want to find the ones that contain the word Tofu. Rather than decompressing the files and then using grep, you can just use zgrep:

```
zgrep Tofu *.food.gz
```

tar — Working with tar archives

The workhorse of LINUX backups, tar is also used as the format for package distribution for Slackware. When picking between tar and cpio, the advantage to tar is that by using the z key tar automatically compresses on backup and decompresses on restore using gzip. The bad news is that tar cannot save and restore special files (like those in /dev). When using tar, the pathnames of files are limited to 100 characters.

LINUXspeak

To create an archive:

tar c[v][z][f *archive*] *files*

To list an archive's table of contents:

tar t[v][z][f *archive*]

To extract from an archive:

tar x [k][m][v][f *archive*] *files*

Key or Argument	Function
f *archive*	Name of the file or device that is the archive. Use - to specify stdin or stdout.
k	Does not overwrite newer files.
m	Preserves file modification time.
v	Verbose — lists filenames or, in the case of table of contents, detailed file information.
z	Compresses files if archiving, decompresses if unarchiving.
files	A list of filenames. If directories are specified, tar descends through the hierarchy, archiving the files within those directories.

For historical reasons, tar treats the command line differently than other LINUX commands do. Make sure that you don't put spaces between the keys or LINUX will most certainly interpret the command incorrectly.

Sample

If you want to back up all the files in the hierarchy under your home directory to a tape (/dev/tape), you can change to your home directory and then enter the following command to create the archive: tar cvf /dev/tape. To verify the contents of the archive, type tar tvf /dev/tape. To extract all the files from the subdirectory Vegetables (not overwriting any newer files), type tar xvfkm /dev/tape Vegetables.

The tar command does offer a way to preserve the last access time of a file, but only using the GNU-style -- option. To preserve the last access time on a file, type --atime-preserve before the filenames. For example, tar xvfkm --atime /dev/tape Vegetables would restore the files from the archive and preserve the last access time.

uuencode — ASCII encoding

Many mailers do not support the transmission of binary files. While MIME attachments offer one means of dealing with transmitting non-ASCII data, uuencode and uudecode are the old standbys of the UNIX world. uuencode converts a file into lines of printable ASCII characters; uudecode decodes the file back into the original binary image.

LINUXspeak

uuencode [-m] [*file*] *name*

Option or Argument	Function
-m	Uses base-64 encoding, commonly used in MIME formats, instead of the uuencode standard.
file	Name of the file to read. stdin is read if you don't specify a file.
name	The name to use in the header of the encoded version of the file.

Sample

Say that you have a big PostScript file and you want to send it to your friend, dopey@snow_white.com. PostScript is just ASCII, so you could simply e-mail the file. If you compress the file, it would be a lot smaller — and therefore easier and quicker to send. The compressed file, however, would not transmit all possible code values for each byte. The answer is to compress the file, uuencode the compressed version, and then mail it. The following shows one of many sequences to accomplish this task:

```
gzip bigfile.ps
uuencode bigfile.ps.gz | mail dopey@snow_white.com
```

uudecode — Decoding ASCII encoding

If you receive a uuencoded file, you can use this command to decode it.

LINUXspeak

```
uudecode [-o outname] [file]
```

Option or Argument	Function
-o outname	Name of the file to create. By default, the name is specified on the first line of the encoded file.
file	Name of the uuencoded file. If not specified, stdin is read.

Sample

Suppose that your friend dopey@snow_white.com has just received this file that claims to be uuencoded. Dopey saves the file as strange_file and now wants to decode it. Dopey enters

```
uudecode strange_file
```

Magically, a new file named bigfile.ps.gz appears in your current directory. You can now decompress the file and print it, using the following code:

```
gunzip bigfile.ps.gz
lpr bigfile.ps
```

uudecode is smart enough to figure out what sort of encoding was used on the file.

zcat — Listing files without decompressing

If you want to list a file that has been compressed with the UNIX compress command or gzip, the command zcat offers an alternative to having to decompress the file and then run an additional command (such as cat) to actually do the intended operation on the file.

LINUXspeak

```
zcat [file]
```

If you don't specify a file, zcat reads from stdin.

Sample

Say that you have all your best vegetarian recipes in a compressed file called healthy_food.gz and you want to take a quick look for your tempeh stew recipe. You can search for a string using less, but less can't read a compressed file. Rather than having to decompress the file, use zcat.

```
zcat healthy_food.gz | less
```

zip and unzip — Working with zip archives

The pkzip command for MS-DOS is a common way to compress and archive files. Functionally, pkzip is equivalent to the LINUX tar command when used with the z key, but the format of a zip archive is not the same as the format of a tar archive. The zip command (which is available for LINUX, UNIX, VMS, MS-DOS, OS/2, Windows NT, Minix, Atari, and Macintosh) offers a way to work with zip format archives. You'll probably use this program when exchanging files with Bill Gates or some of his customers. Those Windows folks probably won't have the capabilities to work with standard tar or cpio files, so you will have to use zip and unzip to exchange files.

LINUXspeak

To create a zip archive or update an archive you use:

```
zip archive list
```

To extract from a zip format archive, you use:

```
unzip archive list
```

Option or Argument	Function
-@	Reads the file names from standard input instead of the command line.
-d	Deletes the files in a list from archive.
-h	Shows a complete list of command line options.
-m	Deletes the original files once the files in a list are added to the archive.
-q	Works silently.
-T	Tests the integrity of the archive.
archive	The name of the archive file. If zip finds that the archive already exists, it adds the files in *list* to the existing archive.
list	A list of filenames to either extract or add to the archive. The default action of $unzip$ is to extract all files in the archive.

Sample

Imagine that Paul Allen sends you a zip archive containing pictures of his new football stadium. You want to retrieve the README.TXT file and the STADIUM.PS file. The archive name is bigdough.zip.

```
unzip bigdough.zip README.TXT STADIUM.PS
```

Creating Schedules and Timed Events

LINUX features some commands that allow you to get your computer to do work for you at a later time (plus a calendar that can save you a lot of paper).

at — Scheduling commands

The at command instructs the computer to do a job at a later time. The job could be as simple as sending you a reminder.

LINUXspeak

```
at [-f file] [-l] [-m] time
```

Argument or Option	Function
-f *file*	Reads commands from *file*. Normally, at expects you to enter the commands from the keyboard and terminate your entry by pressing Ctrl+D.
-l	Just display the at queue (synonym for the atq command).

(continued)

Argument or Option	Function
-m	Mail user when command has been run.
time	Time that you want at to execute the action. You can enter the time in 12-hour format (such as 1145AM or 0930PM), or in 24-hour format (such as 1145 or 2130). If the time has already passed today, tomorrow is assumed. The at command offers many more choices — type man at to see them.

Sample

A simple use for the at command is sending yourself e-mail at a particular time. If you want to send yourself the message at 1:00 p.m., and don't want to include any content in the message, just enter

```
at -m 1300
```

then press Ctrl+D.

You can remove a queued job by using the atrm command (or at -d). Specify the job number as shown by at -l to identify the job you want to delete.

cal — Displaying a calendar

When you see cal, the word *exceptional* doesn't come to mind. But this command does produce a functional calendar for any month or year that you will ever need.

LINUXspeak

cal [[*month*] *year*]

Arguments or Options	Function
month	Number of the month to produce a calendar for. If a month isn't specified, LINUX displays a calendar for the whole year.
year	Year for which you want a calendar (for example, 1998). If you don't specify a year, cal uses the current year.

Sample

Say that your supervisor's birthday is August 11, and you want to know on which day of the week this date falls in 1998. Enter

```
cal 8 1998
```

The cal command produces a calendar for the exact date that you enter. So if you enter a command such as cal 6 98, cal produces a calendar for June of year 98, not June of 1998.

crontab — Scheduling periodic events

LINUX needs to run all sorts of events on a periodic basis and you can use the crontab command to manipulate your schedule for these events. For example, you may need to trim log files, clean out temporary directories, and schedule the execution of your vegetarian mailing-list processing program.

These schedules are saved in /var/spool/cron/crontabs under your user name. The cron daemon (crond) reads these schedule files and starts the requested programs at the requested times.

LINUXspeak
crontab [-d] [-e] [-l] [file]

Argument or Option	Function
-d	Deletes crontab file (the file you tell crontab to install and manipulate).
-e	Edits crontab file by invoking your default text editor on a copy of the file.
-l	Lists crontab file.
file	Name of a file that is to be installed as the new crontab.

Each entry in the crontab file has six fields. The fields are separated by spaces and/or tabs.

Field	Meaning
1	Minute when command is scheduled
2	Hour when command is scheduled
3	Day of month when command is scheduled
4	Month when command is scheduled
5	Day of week when command is scheduled (Sunday is 0, Monday is 1, and so on)
6	Shell command line to be executed

The time fields can contain a comma-delimited list or an * to indicate every time period (every month if in the month field, every day if in the day field, and so on). You can add comment lines to a crontab file by preceding the line with a # character. If you specify both a day of the week and day of the month, the commands are run on the specified weekday, as well as on the specified day of the month.

If the command in `crontab` produces output and you haven't yet written it to a file or sent it to a printer, LINUX e-mails the output to you.

Sample

Suppose that you have a program called get_my_mail, which connects you to the Internet and downloads your mail. Suppose that you want to run this program every two hours during the day (and a couple times during the night) on every weekday. `crontab` can handle this task for you. Assuming that you already have a `crontab` file, enter `crontab -e` to edit your current file and add a line such as this:

```
7 4,8,10,12,14,16,23 * * 1-6 get_my_mail
```

The line above schedules an event to run at 0407, 0807, 1007, 1207, 1407, 1607, and 2307. It is to be run every day of every month on Monday through Saturday (`1-6`). The actual event is to execute the program `get_my_mail`.

All the crontab files are located in /var/spool/cron. Their names are the user IDs of the owner. If you are logged on as root, you can append a user ID to the `crontab` command to list, edit, or delete a user's crontab.

File Management Basics

The commands in this section offer ways to list filenames, access the data within a file, and perform some basic comparisons and manipulations.

cat — Displaying the contents of files

This command gets its name from the word *concatenate,* which means "to link." The `cat` command displays multiple files one after another. Although you can use `cat` to display short files on the screen, `less` is more appropriate to use if your files are longer than a single screen (**see also** "less — Paging through a file" later in this part).

LINUXspeak

`cat` `[-E]` `[-n]` `[-T]` `[-v]` *files*

Option	Function
-E	Shows the ends of lines. Displays a $ after the end of each line.
-n	Adds line numbers to the beginning of each output line.
-T	Displays tab characters as ^I.
-v	Makes nonprintable characters visible by preceding control characters by ^ and preceding characters with the high bit (most significant bit of each character) set with M-. This option is helpful for viewing executable files.

If you type cat (without specifying a filename), LINUX prints whatever characters you type from the keyboard.

Use the -E option to find trailing spaces in lines in a text file. Trailing spaces are a common cause of uneven word spacing when using text formatters such as groff. (*See* Part III.)

Sample

Suppose that you want to print two files for an office mate to look at. You also want to put some instructions on the files as they print so that your office mate knows what to do with the files. Why use a stick-on note when you can include your comments right on the printout without changing the contents of the files? You can add comments easily by using cat.

In the following example, you print the main article from a newsletter, which you want to send to your office mate to receive her feedback. You want her to also look at a new "Green Hat policy." (*See* Part III for information on the lpr command.)

```
cat - main.article - Green.Hat | lpr
Pat, this article looks very interesting, and I
    think it may help with our shortage of wool
    socks.
```

This comment will appear at the top of the newsletter article when it prints out.

The Ctrl+D command sends an End of File to the cat command, telling it that you have finished your input from the keyboard. Now cat puts any further keyboard input at the top of the Green Hat policy when it prints out.

```
Pat -- I really like the idea of wearing a Green
    Hat every Tuesday. Do you think we can get the
    rest of the organization to go along with this?
Ctrl+D
```

Conventions using dash and double dash

UNIX offers single-letter command options that follow a dash (-)
and LINUX continues this tradition. LINUX also offers GNU-style
options for many commands, which consist of two dashes (- -)
followed by a word. For example, if you want to list all the files in a
directory, you can type `ls -a` or `ls --all`. Any command that
supports the GNU-style options should support the `--help`
option. This option instructs the command to display a message
listing all its options, and then exit.

Many commands can read from standard input — either from the
keyboard or from where you have redirected the command (*see*
Part II). Just leaving off a filename or substituting a dash (-) for a
filename usually gets the command to read from standard input.

cp — Copying files and directories

In its simplest form, `cp` copies a file. This command can also copy
a set of files to a new directory.

LINUXspeak

```
cp [-f] [-i] [-p] [-R] [-v] source_file
    destination_file
cp [-f] [-i] [-p] [-R] [-v] source_files directory
```

Option	Function
-f	Forces overwriting existing destination files.
-i	Interactively prompts whether to overwrite an existing file.
-p	Preserves the original file characteristics including owner, permissions, and last modify time.
-R	Recursively copies directories as well as regular files.
-u	Overwrites a file only if the file being copied is newer than the destination file. Turns `cp` into a mini-archiver.
-v	Verbose mode. Prints the name of each file as it is copied.

Sample

You want to make a copy of your recipe files so you can update
them to HTML without disturbing the originals. The recipe files are
in your home directory and you want to make the copies in a new
directory called `Html`. If all your recipes have `.food` at the end of
the filename, type

```
cp *.food ~/Html/
```

less — Paging through a file

The less command when invoked with nothing more than a filename displays the file a page at a time on the screen.

LINUXspeak

less [-p *pattern*] *files*

Option	Function
-p *pattern*	Starts displaying from the first line that contains the *pattern*

Sample

Suppose that you keep a file of all the checks you've written, which is sorted by date. If you want to view the checks file starting at 10-11-97, you type

less -p 10-11-97 checks

Don't forget that the shell has its own special meaning for some characters such as *. If you think that your pattern may be special to the shell, it's always safest to quote it.

Many search options are built into less. The most common option is to search forward for a particular word after you have entered the less command line. To do this, press /, type the pattern, and press Enter. Type NB if you want to repeat the previous search.

To discover a complete list of less options and commands, type less -h, or just press h if you're already in less rather than being at your shell prompt.

ls — Displaying filenames and information

Each file has a name and some characteristics associated with the file, including its size in bytes, various dates of modification, owner, and permissions (**see** the "Using Attributes and Permissions" section later in this part). The ls command displays this information in a variety of formats that you select using the command line options.

LINUXspeak

ls [-a] [-F] [-i] [-l] [-r] [-R] [-t] [-u]
    [*pathnames*]

Option	Function
-a	Includes all files and directories in the listing, including those with names starting with a dot.
-F	Appends a character to each filename to indicate its type: * for executable regular files, / for directories, @ for symbolic links, | for FIFOs, and = for sockets.
-i	Includes the *inode* number (internal file number) in the display. This option is useful if you want to see if filenames are synonyms. If the inode numbers are the same and the files are in the same file system, they are just different names for the same file (**see also** "ln — Creating multiple names for a file," later in this part).
-l	Displays a long listing of file information, including permissions, size, owner, and modification time.
-r	Reverses the order of the sort (the default sort order is alphabetical).
-R	Recursively accesses files in any subdirectories.
-t	Sorts the listing by last modification time.
-u	Sorts the listing by last access time.

Sample

Determining which files have been most recently modified is very handy. If you want a long list of files (-l), including hidden files (-a), sorted in reverse order (-r) by last modification time (-t), use following command.

```
ls -latr
```

You can list all the files that have names starting with a particular character by using a wildcard (**see** Part II). For example, to display information on all files with names starting with an r in /usr/bin, type

```
ls /usr/bin/r*
```

The ls command contains a wide assortment of options. The preceding table lists those used most often. For a full list of options in a format similar to that table, type ls --help, and then press Enter. This command instructs the ls command to print a help message explaining all the possible options.

The ls command normally lists the files in directories, rather than just the directory name itself. Use the -d option to tell ls to list just the directories without their contents.

mv — Moving a file

Use the mv command to move a file to a new location or to change the name of a file. If the source and destination are on the same file system, mv simply renames the file. If source and destination are on different file systems, the source file is copied to the destination and then the source file is deleted. If the last argument given to mv is a directory, mv decides that the other arguments are the names of files that should be moved to this destination directory.

LINUXspeak

```
mv [-f] [-i] [-v] source_file destination_file
mv [-f] [-i] [-v] source_files directory
```

Option or Argument	Function
-f	Forced overwriting of destination files.
-i	Interactive move. mv prompts before each move is attempted and waits for the user to press y or Y.
-v	Verbose. Prints the name of each file before moving it.
source_files	Files to be moved
destination_file	Location where the file is to be moved.
directory	Directory where all source files are to be moved.

Sample

Suppose that you have a recipe named tofu_curry.food, but you realize that the recipe is actually for tempeh curry. To change the name of the file to be more appropriate, you enter

```
mv tofu_curry.food tempeh_curry.food
```

Now suppose that you have all your recipes named correctly, and you want to move the files to a new directory. The following code creates a directory named GoodFood, and then moves all the recipes over to it.

```
mv *.food GoodFood
```

Online Documentation

Beyond the boundaries of this book you can find online documentation that may supply additional useful information.

info — Displaying GNU-style online documentation

info is the GNU hypertext documentation system. This system allows you to view documents on-screen or print the documentation. You can perform on-screen viewing using the info program or within Emacs.

My personal experience with info has been one of confusion and frustration — the documentation doesn't seem to match all the capabilities of the command — however, a lot of documentation is available in info format in /usr/info. If you decide info is what you like but don't like the info program, try the info mode in Emacs or check your LINUX distribution for GUI-based info readers.

info uses a tree of files, each containing nodes to access the information. The default location for this tree is /usr/info.

LINUXspeak
info [-f *file*] [-h] [-n *node*] [-o *outfile*]

Argument or Option	Function
-f *file*	File to open when info starts (dir default).
-h	Displays help message and exits.
-n *node*	Node to locate (top of the tree default).
-o *outfile*	Output file. By default, is info interactive and sends output back to the screen.

After you are running info, a whole assortment of commands are available to move around. Just type h for details.

man — The Old Faithful of Documentation

man has been the standard format for UNIX documentation for more than 25 years. man (short for *manual*) is actually the name of a macro package for the groff text formatting system. man is also the name of a command that displays documents that are in man format on screen.

LINUXspeak
man [*section*] *command*
man -k *keyword*

Argument or Option	Function
command	The name of the command whose documentation you want to display.
section	The number of the manual section to search (by default, man search all sections).
	1 — commands
	2 — system calls
	3 — library functions
	4 — devices
	5 — files
	6 — games
	7 — miscellaneous
	8 — systems administration
	n — Tcl/Tk
-k keyword	Use this option if you don't know which command you want. This option searches the whatis database (for details, type man whatis) and returns the names and synopses of commands that match your keyword.

The man command is highly configurable. Take a look at /etc/man.config for a well-commented description of the configuration of man on your system. If you still have questions, use man — after all, that's what it is for. Just enter man man.

Sample

You know that there must be some command that displays CPU utilization, but you have no idea what command it may be. Enter

```
man -k cpu
```

On my system, I get two matches — one about ncpumount and one about top.

```
ncpumount (8)  - unmount a NetWare filesystem
    mounted with ncpmount.
top (1)     - display top CPU processes
```

The description of top is *display top CPU processes*. This sounds good, so to get the details on top, you enter

```
man top
```

The output of man includes a synopsis section, a command description showing all the available options and arguments, and a description of any possible problems or bugs.

If man -k doesn't return any results, it is possible that the whatis database used by man -k hasn't been built. As root, enter /sbin/ makewhatis to recreate the database.

/usr/doc — Finding online documentation

The /usr/doc directory is a repository for all the latest documentation on the LINUX system and LINUX commands. This directory contains no specific programs, but if you are looking for additional information on a command or feature, check out this directory. It is organized with a subdirectory name for each command and, within those subdirectories, descriptive text files.

Printing

When you ask LINUX to print a file, the file is spooled in a directory and then queued for a printer (called a *print spooling system*). If multiple print jobs are queued, LINUX handles the print jobs sequentially. This section covers the commands that spool print jobs and work with the spool queues, plus it covers how you format documents into pages and display, or print, PostScript files.

gv — Displaying PostScript files

GhostScript is a PostScript translator that is included with LINUX. GhostScript is capable of printing PostScript files on non PostScript printers. gv is a front end for GhostScript that runs under X and allows you to view the pages of a PostScript document on the screen. If gv isn't available in your menus under X, just enter gv in a shell window to bring it up.

LINUXspeak

gv [-magstep *n*] [-h] [-*psize*] [-landscape]
    [*filename*]

Argument or Option	Function
-h	Displays a table of all available command line options.
-landscape	Sets display to landscape mode.
-magstep *n*	Sets magnification. Valid values depend on the page size.
-*psize*	Specifies page size. Valid values include letter, tabloid, legal, a4, a5, and b5.

Sample

Suppose you have a picture of the Grateful Dead that is in PostScript format and saved in a file named gd.ps. To display the file in landscape mode, type `gv -landscape gd.ps`.

lpq — Examining the print queue

You can check the status of a particular job (or all jobs) in the print queue by using the `lpq` command.

LINUXspeak

`lpq [-l] [-P printer] [users]`

Option or Argument	Function
-l	Prints detailed information about each file in a print job.
-P printer	Displays information about files in the queue for printer. The default action is to display information about the default print queue (or if set, the queue associated with the environment variable PRINTER setting).
users	Displays only print jobs for specified users. The default is all print jobs.

Sometimes, you may see (standard input) — with the parentheses included — listed as the filename in the print queue. This really isn't weird, it just means that you used `lpr` at the end of a pipeline, so there really wasn't a file. `lpr` just creates its own temporary file and queues it.

Sample

Assume that you queued a print job to the `fancy` printer some time ago, and you still don't have the output. The following command displays information about all jobs queued to that printer and shows your status in the print queue.

`lpq -P fancy`

lpr — Queuing print requests

The `lpr` command places print jobs in the print queue.

LINUXspeak

`lpr [-#num] [-h] [-m] [-p] [-P printer] files`

Option or Argument	Function
-#*num*	Prints *num* copies.
-h	Does not print a header page.
-m	Sends e-mail when the print job is complete.
-p	Formats the files using the pr program. (**See** "pr — Formatting files into pages" later in this section.)
-P *printer*	Place this job in the queue for printer called *printer*.
files	Specifies names of files to be queued for printing.

Sample

Say that you have a couple files called spinach_salad.txt and lentil_salad.txt, which you want to print on the fancy printer (appropriately named fancy). Because fancy is not in your office, you want to get e-mail when the print jobs are done. The following command queues the print jobs and requests e-mail when each job completes.

```
lpr -P fancy -m spinach_salad.txt lentil_salad.txt
```

lprm — Removing queued print jobs

With lprm, you can remove any jobs you have queued for print. root can remove any queued print job.

LINUXspeak

```
lprm [-P printer] [jobs] [user]
```

Option or Argument	Function
-P *printer*	Removes jobs from the queue for *printer*
jobs	A list of job numbers to remove (use lpq to get the job numbers; **see also** "lpq — Examine the print queue")
user	Removes print jobs queued by *user* (option available to superuser only)

Sample

Suppose your login name is laurie and you want to display information about all the print jobs you have queued. Type lpq laurie.

pr — Formatting files into pages

While you can send almost anything to the printer with lpr, you won't necessarily have logical page breaks, headings, and dates. The pr command adds these and other types of formatting to your output.

LINUXspeak

pr [+*num*] [-*cols*] [-c] [-d] [-f] [-h *hdr*] [-l *lines*] [-m] [-o *width*] [-t] *files*

Option or Argument	Function
+*num*	Discards output before page *num*.
-*cols*	Formats output into *cols* columns.
-c	Displays control characters as a caret (^) followed by the printable character (for example, Ctrl+X is displayed as ^X).
-d	Double space output.
-f	Separates pages with formfeeds, not newlines.
-h *hdr*	Use *hdr* as the page header text instead of the name of the file. Don't forget to quote *hdr* if it contains white space or other characters of interest to the shell.
-l *lines*	Sets page length to *lines* (default is 66 lines).
-m	Prints each file in their own column.
-o *width*	Sets the left margin to *width* characters.
-t	Suppresses page headers and footers. Normally, LINUX prints a page header that includes the filename, date, time, and page number.
files	Names of the files to print.

More often than not, you should include the -f option with the pr command. Instead of the LINUX system having to insert the exact number of lines to get to the end of the page, pr -f just sends a formfeed when it wants to skip to the next page.

Sample

Suppose that you have two lists, one called good and one called bad. You want to print them out, side by side, with a title of "Good and Bad List," and a ten-character left margin. Just enter the following:

```
pr -f -h "Good and Bad List" -m -o 10 good bad |
    lpr
```

Sorting and Searching

In this section, I show you the commands that can be used to locate a file and search for information within a file, and how to sort data.

find — Locating a file that meets specified characteristics

The find command searches the specified paths for files that match the specified selection criteria. This command is known for having the worst syntax in LINUX, but this reputation is because of the number of files that you can specify. The following information is only a small subset of what find can do. Type find --help to print a usage message (a message which is, at best, confusing.) **See also** the man page (enter man find) for more information on find.

LINUXspeak

find [*paths*] [*expressions*]

Option or Argument	Function
paths	Any number of locations in the file hierarchy tree where find should start its search
expressions	Find criteria

The following table shows the expressions you can use with the find command.

Expression Choices	What They Mean
-name *name*	Finds files whose names match *name*. You can use regular expressions if you quote them.
-newer *name*	Finds files that have been modified more recently than file *name*.
-perm mode	Finds files whose permissions exactly match mode (octal).
-perm -*mode*	Finds files with a permission bitmask that has all bits also set in *mode*.
-user *uname*	Finds files owned by *uname*.
-exec *command*	Passes *command* to the shell for execution. Use »{ }« to specify the currently matching filename and \ ; to terminate the object of the exec.
-print	Prints the names of each matching file.

Sample

You have a bunch of files with names ending in .bak in your directory hierarchy and you want to delete them. Assuming that you are in your home directory, use the following code:

```
find . -name "*.bak" -exec rm "{}" \;
```

+ The double quotes are necessary to prevent the shell from interpreting the strings inside. Without the quotes around *.bak, the shell would expand the string to match all files whose names ended with .bak in the current directory. Thus, the find command would miss the files from any subdirectories.

+ The braces also have special meaning to the shell but, if they make their way to the find command, the braces are replaced with the currently matching filename.

+ The backslash in front of the semicolon means find will see this character and interpret it as the end of the arguments to find.

find has other capabilities:

+ Matching on file size

+ Matching type of file

+ Determining last time a file was accessed or modified

+ Providing ownership information

grep — Looking for patterns in files

The grep command displays lines of files that contain a specified pattern. (**See also** Part X of this book.)

LINUXspeak

```
grep [-num] [-c] [-f file] [-i] [-l] [-n] [-v] [-w]
     [-x] [-e] pattern files
```

Option or Argument	Function
-num	Displays num lines before and after the matching line so you can see the context of the match
-c	Prints a count of the matching lines in each file instead of the matching lines
-f file	Retrieves the pattern from file
-i	Ignores case when matching pattern with input data

(continued)

Option or Argument	Function
-l	Prints the names of files that contain matches only, not the matching lines
-n	Adds line numbers to the beginning of the output records
-v	Selects nonmatching lines instead of matching ones
-w	Performs the match on whole words, not substrings
-x	Selects only if the pattern matches the whole line
-e	Used in front of a pattern that starts with a - to prevent grep from interpreting the pattern as an option
pattern	A regular expression to match

Sample

Say that you have a data file that is supposed to be composed of lines that contain e-mail addresses, but some lines contain data other than e-mail addresses. You know that all e-mail addresses contain an at sign (@) and you want to display a list of the bad lines. You enter

```
grep -v @ data_file
```

A common situation is to look for something at the beginning of a line. The caret (^) character anchors the search to the beginning of the line. You can easily perform a "beginning of line match" by prefixing your search pattern with a ^.

locate — Finding files quickly

Use a database of file locations to quickly find files whose names match the criteria you specify.

LINUXspeak

```
locate [-d path] patterns
```

Option or Argument	Function
-d *path*	Uses filename databases in *path* instead of the default databases. *path* is a colon-separated list.
patterns	In the simplest form, a list of strings to search for as part of a filename in the database. The patterns can contain shell-style metacharacters: *, ? and [ ]. Because the shell normally interprets the metacharacters, you must quote the pattern if it contains any of these characters.

Sample

Suppose you know that some HTML documents are out on the system, but you are not sure where. The following `locate` does a quick and dirty search for them.

```
locate html
```

Chances are that you got too many matches. You can refine your search a little if you know that the filenames also contain the word food.

```
locate "food*html"
```

sort — Sorting data

You can use `sort` to sort, merge, or compare files.

LINUXspeak

```
sort [-m] [-sortorder] [-k pos1[,pos2] [-o outfile]
     [-t separator] [-u] files
```

Option or Argument	Function
-m	Merges all input files into one sorted output file.
-sortorder	Affects how all sort keys (fields) are interpreted. Use the following letters in place of the *sortorder* variable:
	b — ignores leading blanks
	d — sorts in alphabetical order ignoring punctuation
	f — folds lowercase into uppercase
	i — ignores nonprintable characters
	M — treats the key as three-letter month abbreviation
	n — compares arithmetically
	r — sorts in reverse order
-k pos1[,pos2]	Specifies the sort fields. *pos1* specifies the field used to start the key (the first field is numbered 1) and *pos2* is the last field to use.
-o outfile	Specifies the name of the output file. It is permissible to specify a file for *outfile* that is one of the input files.
-t separator	Sets the field separator character to *separator*. Tab is the default.
-u	Deletes the duplicate if a like occurs multiple times
files	Specifies the files to be sorted.

Sample

Suppose that you want to perform an alphabetical sort on a file whose lines contain a last name, a comma, and first name. While you could treat the name as two sort fields (last name and first name), this isn't necessary. The comma character sorts before any letter, so Smith, Joe will appear before Smithe, Anne. If the name of the data file is people and you want the output directed to the file called people.sorted, either of the following commands would do it. The first command uses output redirection and the second uses the -o option to specify the output file.

```
sort people >people.sorted
sort -o people.sorted people
```

The second form in the preceding example (using the -o option) allows you to save the output in the same file as the input. However, *do not* use the -o option with shell redirection. The shell interprets the redirection first — so, in the process of creating the output file, the shell would overwrite your data file before the sort is executed.

If you're familiar with UNIX, you can see that the way LINUX interprets the field numbers with the -k option is different from the traditional way to specify fields with UNIX sort. The reason for the change is POSIX compliance. If you are an old UNIX user, the other format still works.

Using Attributes and Permissions

Every file and directory has ownership information and access permissions associated with them that can be modified.

chgrp — Changing the group of a file

If you only want to change the group ID of a file, you can use the chgrp command instead of chown.

LINUXspeak

chgrp [-R] *group files*

Option or Argument	Function
-R	Recursively changes ownership of directories and their contents
group	New group ID for the files

chmod — Changing file access permissions

LINUX is a multi-user system — it offers file permissions associated with the owner of the file, the group the file is in, and anyone who is not the file owner or the group associated with the file. You use the chmod command to change the permissions of an existing file.

Two ways exist to use chmod: symbolic (such as r for read) or octal. An octal digit contains three bits. Because the permissions are grouped into three 3-bit segments, I personally prefer octal numbers.

LINUXspeak

chmod [-R] *mode files*

Option or Argument	Function
-R	Recursively changes permissions of directories and their contents
mode	Accesses permissions in octal or symbolically
files	A list of files whose permissions you are changing

The symbolic specification is made up of three parts — each of which is optional. The parts of the symbolic specification are

+ **The type of ownership:** u for user, g for group, o for other, or a for all

+ **An operator:** + for add permissions, - for remove permissions, or = for set permissions exactly as specified

+ **The values to set:** r for read, w for write, and x for execute or directory search.

If you need to specify more than one symbolic specification, use a command to separate the specifications.

Using octal, the following values are added together to form the bitmap.

Value	Meaning
4000	Set user ID on execute
2000	Set group ID on execute
1000	For directories, only file owner can create/delete files
400	Owner read

Value	Meaning
200	Owner write
100	Owner execute
40	Group read
20	Group write
10	Group execute
4	Other read
2	Other write
1	Other execute

Generally, you should specify execute permission for any file that is to be directly executed. This includes compiled programs and shell scripts. You should also specify execute permission for a directory — this allows the directory to be searched.

Sample

Suppose that you want to add group write permission and remove read for other from all the .txt files in your current directory. The current permissions are read/write for owner (400 for owner read, 200 for owner write) and read only for group (40) and other (4), which adds up to octal 644. Using the symbolic way to specify the command, you enter the following:

```
chmod g+w,o-r *.txt
```

Sample output of the ls -l command would look like this:

```
total 33
drwxr-xr-x 2 fyl users 1024 Jan 7 1996 Boston/
drwxr-xr-x 2 fyl users 1024 Aug 29 07:42 IDG/
drwxr-xr-x 2 fyl users 1024 Apr 17 09:16 Series/
-rw-rw-r-- 1 fyl users 4909 Apr 16 21:10 embed.mm
-rw-r--r-- 1 fyl users   77 Apr 14 19:53 kern-find
-rw-r--r-- 1 fyl users  348 Apr 15 14:36 me
-rw-rw-r-- 1 fyl users 21091 Apr 16 21:11
   ose.ovhd.mm
-rw-r--r-- 1 fyl users  309 Jun 19 1996 vil
-rw-r--r-- 1 fyl users    0 Sep 2 16:32 xx
```

The first character of the lines indicates the type of file (d for directory, - for regular file). The next nine characters of the lines are the file permissions. The directories have permissions of 755 (rwx for owner, r-x for group and other), the next file 664 (rw- for owner and group, r-- for other) the next 644 (rw- for owner, r-- for group and other), and so on.

chown — Changing the owner of a file

Each file has an owner and also belongs in a particular group. You can change either (use . *group* to change group only) or both using the chown command.

You can change the ownership of a file only if you logged on as root.

LINUXspeak

chown [-R] [*user*][.][*group*] *files*

Option or Argument	Function
-R	Recursively changes ownership of directories and their contents
user	New user ID for the files
group	New group ID for the files

Sample

Say that you have permission to log on as root and you want to make a copy of your recipe files for your new user, Donnie. A good place for these files from your Good_Food directory is in a similar directory in Donnie's hierarchy.

```
cd Good_Food
su
mkdir ~donnie/Good_Food
cp * ~donnie/Good_Food
chown -R donnie ~donnie/Good_Food
exit
```

While the above example works, a safer way to do this would be to make your files available for read by Donnie and let Donnie make the directory and copy the files. As a general rule, do all you can to avoid being logged on as root, a situation in which a simple mistake can have much more impact than if you were just logged on as a user.

umask — Changing your default file creation mask

When you run a program that creates a file, that program requests certain permissions. For example, a text editor normally asks for read/write permission for everyone (user, group, and other), and a program that is building an executable program would also ask for execute permission. The permissions received are limited by the value of your umask. Any bit set in a umask corresponds to a permission that is not granted. For example, if your umask is set to

0, nothing is limited, and all permissions asked for are granted. Each bit set in umask means that you will not get that permission in the file that you create.

LINUXspeak
umask [*ovalue*]

Option or Argument	Function
ovalue	Octal value specifying the permissions that won't be granted when a program requests a new file to be created. If not specified, umask just displays the current value of your umask.

Sample
If you generally want to deny group write to your files and any access by others, you need to look up the bits that correspond to these permissions. These bits, expressed in octal, are 20 for write by group, 1 for execute by other, 2 for write by other and 4 for read by other. Adding these values results in a umask setting like this:

umask 027

Working with Directories and Disks

The commands in this section enable you to see what is available in terms of disk space, move around in the file hierarchy, and work with directories.

cd — Changing directories

The following command changes the current directory to the directory that you specify. If no directory is specified after cd (the brackets around *directory* indicate that it is optional), LINUX moves you to your home directory.

LINUXspeak
cd [*directory*]

cd - changes back to the previous directory.

When you create a directory (with mkdir), LINUX adds two filenames to the directory — dot (.) and double dot (..) — that are links. These filenames are the synonym for your current directory and the parent of your current directory, respectively. One of the handiest uses for .. is in conjunction with the cd command. To change back to your parent directory, just type

cd ..

The most common use of . is in the cp command. If you are copying something to your current directory, you can use . as the destination.

Another handy shortcut with cd is the hyphen (-). To return to the most recent directory you were in, just type cd – and then press Enter.

df — Displaying free disk space

The df command shows the amount of free space in a file system. By default it provides information on all the mounted file systems but you can modify what information is displayed.

LINUXspeak

df [-k] [-t *fstype*] [-x *fstype*] [*filesystems*]

Option or Argument	Function
-k	Displays sizes in kilobytes instead of 512-byte blocks
-t *fstype*	Displays information only for filesystems of type *fstype*
-x *fstype*	Displays information for filesystems of all types except *fstype*
filesystems	Selects file systems you want included in the output (default is all mounted file systems)

Sample

Suppose that you have a second hard disk (/dev/hdb). If you want to see how much free space exists on its two LINUX partitions, 1 and 3, type

df /dev/hdb1 /dev/hdb3

du — Showing used disk space

The disk usage command (du) shows summary information of how much space is used by the contents of each directory in the file hierarchy.

LINUXspeak

du [-a] [-b] [-c] [-D] [-k] [-s] [-S] [*directories*]

Option or Argument	Function
-a	Displays counts for all files, not just directories
-b	Displays the sizes in bytes (512-byte blocks default)
-c	Displays a grand total for all command line arguments
-D	Dereferences symbolic links that are command line arguments
-k	Displays sizes in kilobytes
-s	Displays only a total for each argument
-S	Counts the size of each directory separately rather than including the sizes of its subdirectories

Sample

Say that you have a bunch of subdirectories in your home directory and want to get an idea how much space is used in each subdirectory. From your home directory, type the following:

du

Too simple? Maybe you want to know how big all the subdirectories of /usr are. Type

du /usr

 On many systems, /tmp is a symbolic link to /var/tmp. A command such as du /tmp only displays the size of the link, not the size of the actual directory contents. You can use du -D /tmp to see actual usage for this directory.

mkdir — Creating new directories

The mkdir command creates one or more directories. It also allows you to set the access permissions of the directories when they are created.

LINUXspeak

mkdir [-m *mode*] [-p] *directories*

Option	Function
-m *mode*	Sets directory permissions to a particular mode (**see also** "chmod — Changing file access permissions" for details on mode values)
-p	Creates any missing parent directories

Sample

Suppose that you want to create a pair of directories off your home directory called Good_food and Bad_food. You also want everyone to have read permission and execute (search) permission to these directories. However, you want to allow write permission only for yourself. Just type the following:

```
Mkdir -m 755 ~/Good_food ~/Bad_food
```

pwd — Displaying the current directory location

The pwd command displays your current directory. Most shells have built-in versions of this command, which saves loading time.

rmdir — Removing an empty directory

Use the rmdir command to remove empty directories. If you want to remove a directory and its contents, *see* the section "rm — Deleting files" later in this part.

LINUXspeak

```
rmdir [-p] directories
```

Option	Function
-p	Removes any parent directories that are explicitly mentioned in an argument if they become empty after the specified directories are removed

Working with File Content

Sometimes you want a program to tell you about the content of a file without having to look at the contents yourself.

file — Describing the contents of a file

The file command uses a table (located in /etc/magic) to help it determine what sort of file you have. If file says that your file is text, it is probably safe to edit the file or display what's in it using less. If the file command indicates that your file contains executable code, od is the right tool if you want to display the content of the file.

LINUXspeak

```
file files
```

Sample

If you have a directory with an assortment of files and want to
know what they contain, type `file *.` for a result like this:

```
12786vaa.html: ascii text
Deb:     directory
Pt1-2.zip:  zip archive file - version 2.0
XCalendar:  English text
data.tar.gz:  gzip compressed data - deflate method
ed.a02279:  empty
fig4-10.tif:  TIFF file, little-endian version 42
nvi:     Bourne Shell script text
part1:    ascii text
passwd:    ELF 32-bit LSB executable i386
qmark.xbm:  c program text
```

fmt — Adjusting line lengths

This command is a simple formatter that inserts or deletes line
breaks (newlines) to make all lines approximately the same length.
`fmt` breaks lines between words so that the lines do not exceed a
specified length.

LINUXspeak

`fmt [-len] [files]`

Option or Argument	Function
`-len`	Sets the maximum line length to *len* (72 default)
`files`	Inputs files to read
`stdin`	Reads from standard input if no files specified

Sample

The most common use of `fmt` is within the vi editor. To move the
line breaks of a paragraph within vi, move the cursor to the top of
a paragraph, type `!}fmt`, and then press Enter.

head — Displaying the first part of files

The `head` command displays the specified portion (ten lines is the
default) of the indicated files starting at the beginning of each one.
If multiple filenames are specified, each file's printed lines have a
source filename, bracketed by `==>` on the left and `<==` on the right
side of the filename.

LINUXspeak

`head [-c bc] [-b lc] files`

Option	Function
-c *bc*	Displays the first *bc* bytes (*bc* being a number count). *bc* may be followed by b to multiply the count by 512 (blocks), k for kilobytes, or m for megabytes.
-n *lc*	Displays the first *lc* lines. This option can also be written as simply *-lc*.
-q	Doesn't print filename headers.
stdin	Reads from standard input if no files specified.

Sample

Suppose that you have a bunch of meeting agendas, and in the first line of each agenda is a brief description of the meeting topic. You can use head to make a list of these meeting agendas and their brief descriptions. If the agendas are in your current directory, and their names end with .meet, type

```
head -1 *.meet
```

To print this listing, type

```
head -1 *.meet | lpr
```

ln — Creating multiple names for a file

The ln command adds a new name to a file, also known as a *link*. It can also create multiple links that appear in a particular directory. (For more information on using ln, **see** the on-line pages by entering man ln.)

LINUXspeak

```
ln [-f] [-s] pathname
ln [-f] [-s] filename newfilename
ln [-f] [-s] filenames directory
```

Option or Argument	Function
-f	Forces creation of the link even if *newfilename* exists.
-s	Creates a symbolic link (pointer) instead of a hard link.
pathname	The name of an existing file in another directory. LINUX creates a file with an identical name in the current directory.
filename	The name of an existing file.
newfilename	The name of the new link.
directory	The directory where you want the new link(s) to appear.

Sample

Pretend that you have a file in your current directory called my_life. You realize that some people won't know who the file refers to. To add a second name to use to reference this file type

```
ln my_life marys_life
```

Suppose that on your system, there is a directory called /hard/to/ remember/where that contains some files that you use all the time. You decide you want these files to be available to you in /home/ me/Links. You must type

```
cd /hard/to/remember/where
ln /home/me/Links
```

Or, you can type

```
ln /hard/to/remember/where/* /home/me/Links
```

rm — Deleting files

The most potentially dangerous of all file commands is the one that makes files go away. LINUX is a multitasking operating system, which means that another task could grab the disk space you just freed up. So you may not always recover a file that you accidentally deleted.

LINUXspeak

```
rm [-f] [-i] [-r] files
```

Option or Argument	Function
-f	Forces the file removal.
-i	Interactively prompts before removing each file. If you type a word beginning with y or Y, the file is removed.
-r	Remove the contents of the directories recursively.

The -r option can be dangerous. If you're logged on as root and in the root directory, you could remove all the files on your system if you're not careful.

Sample

If you want to delete all the files in your current directory having names ending with .bak type

```
rm -i *.bak
```

You can use the echo command to check what will happen with an rm command before you execute the command. Type echo, followed by the pattern that you plan to use to remove files. LINUX displays a list of the candidate files. If the list looks good, simply use your history mechanism in the following list to retrieve the command and replace echo with rm.

✦ If your shell is set in Emacs mode, the key sequence to retrieve the command is Ctrl+P, Ctrl+A, Alt+M. Then type rm and press Enter.

✦ If your shell is in vi mode, the sequence is Esc, K, cw, rm. Then press Enter.

Removing a file that has some strange characters in its name presents a common LINUX problem. These strange characters may be control characters. Or, you may have a filename that starts with a dash (-), so rm thinks that you are trying to pass it an option. You can use ./ in front of the name to deal with a leading dash and you can use wildcards in combination with the -i option to home in on the right name for the file.

tail — Accessing the last part of files

Sometimes the information that you need is at the end of a file. tail displays the last portion of a file.

LINUXspeak
tail [-c *bc*] [-b *lc*] *files*

Option or Argument	Function
-c *bc*	Displays the last *bc* bytes. *bc* may be followed by b to multiply the count by 512 (blocks), k for kilobytes, or m for megabytes.
-f	Follows the flow of input. After printing out the last portion of the file, tail continues to run while it waits for lines to be added to the file by another program. When lines are added, tail displays them.
-n *lc*	Displays the last *lc* lines.
-q	Doesn't print filename headers.

tail reads stdin (keyboard input) if it's run with a - (hyphen) or if no files are specified.

If you have a report program running and you want to see how it is progressing run tail -f on its output or log file and you will see the new output lines as they appear.

wc — Counting words, lines, and characters

wc counts the number of words, lines, and characters in a file. The command then displays all three counts, along with the filename by default. If multiple files appear on the command line, LINUX also displays a grand total.

LINUXspeak

wc [-c] [-l] [-w] *files*

Option	Function
-c	Displays the number of characters in the file
-l	Displays the number of lines in the file
-w	Displays the number of words in the file
files	Files to read and count.
stdin	Reads from standard input if - or no files are specified

Sample

Suppose that you have a set of recipe files and you want to know how many lines are in each file and the total number of lines in every file. If these files are in your current directory, and their names end with .food, type wc -l *.food, and then press Enter.

Working with the System

This section covers how you interact with the operating system — how to terminate a shell, change your password, find out which processes end users are currently running, and how to add and remove file systems.

exit — Leaving a shell

When you log on, you enter a shell. You can enter subshells by running shell scripts or by typing the name of a shell as a command. The exit command instructs your current shell to terminate. If you leave your login shell, you log off. You can optionally specify a return value (0–255) for the exiting shell to return as its exit status.

LINUXspeak

exit [*value*]

Argument	Function
value	You can pass a value back to the calling shell by setting *value*. By convention, zero indicates success and nonzero values are used to indicate a particular type of failure.

All commands return an exit status. You can display the current exit status by echoing the current value of the exit status variable. The Bourne shell and its relatives store this value in $?. C Shell relatives store it in $status. Remember, every command returns a status, so after you have read the status you have changed its meaning to the success or failure of the command that read it. If you need to use the status value more than once, the first thing you need to do is save the value in another shell variable.

finger — *Checking up on users*

The finger command displays information about a specified user or all users on either your local machine or a specified machine. If you finger an individual user, the user's current login status and the contents of the user's .plan file is displayed. If you finger a computer (for example, finger @a42.com), finger shows the status of everyone currently logged in.

LINUXspeak

finger [-l] [-m] [-p] [-s] [*what*]

You can use the finger command locally or over a network.

Argument or Option	Function
-l	Displays the long format of finger information (default for finger of one user).
-m	Only matches login names — doesn't attempt to match *what* to a user's name.
-p	Doesn't display .plan and .project files.
-s	Displays the short format of finger information (default for finger of an entire machine).
what	A login name, machine name in the form @machine, or login and machine name in the form user@machine. If omitted, information on all users on the current machine is displayed.

Sample

Suppose that you want to find out if your friend Ellen is logged on to her machine. You know that her machine is uncle.ssc.com, and her login is emd. You can finger her computer with either of the following commands:

```
finger emd@uncle.ssc.com
finger ellen@uncle.ssc.com
```

The output from typing finger on one of my computers looks like this.

```
Login Name      Tty Idle Login Time Office   Office
    Phone
fyl   Phil Hughes    1 21d Oct  3 06:49
fyl   Phil Hughes   p0   Oct  3 06:49 (:0.0)
fyl   Phil Hughes   p2 23:11 Oct 18 21:55 (:0.0)
fyl   Phil Hughes   p3  1 Oct  4 09:55 (:0.0)
```

Here is the output from typing finger fyl on the same system.

```
Login: fyl               Name: Phil Hughes
Directory: /home/fyl     Shell: /bin/bash
On since Fri Oct  3 06:49 (PST) on tty1 21 days 2
    hours idle
On since Fri Oct  3 06:49 (PST) on ttyp0 from :0.0
On since Sat Oct 18 21:55 (PST) on ttyp2 from :0.0
 23 hours 11 minutes idle
On since Sat Oct  4 09:55 (PST) on ttyp3 from :0.0
 1 minute 26 seconds idle
No mail.
Plan:
My plan is the same as all LINUX users: World
    Domination.
```

One of the pieces of information displayed by finger is the contents of the .plan file in your home directory. If you want people to know something, .plan is a good place to put it, but not a good place to save your secrets.

mount — Mounting filesystems

You can use the mount command to make additional devices and disk partitions available, as well as CD-ROMs. The superuser can mount arbitrary devices, but ordinary users are limited to mounting things that the superuser has permitted.

LINUXspeak

```
mount [node]
umount [node]
```

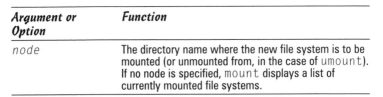

Argument or Option	Function
node	The directory name where the new file system is to be mounted (or unmounted from, in the case of umount). If no node is specified, mount displays a list of currently mounted file systems.

To allow users to mount file systems, add an entry in /etc/fstab for the desired mount point and device and add the keyword user to the fourth field. (*See Linux Secrets* [IDG Books Worldwide, Inc.] for more details on /etc/fstab.)

Sample

Your system has two user-mountable filesystems in /etc/fstab:

- ✦ /cdrom for mounting CDs

- ✦ /A for mounting MS-DOS floppy disks on the first floppy drive

Assume that you want to mount a CD and an MS-DOS floppy and copy the file cool.stf from the CD to the floppy. Use the following sequence:

```
mount /A
mount /cdrom
cp /cdrom/cool.stf /A/
umount /A
umount /cdrom
```

passwd — Changing your password

Choose a password carefully and don't make it available to anyone else. Recent passwd programs do some checks to make sure that your password isn't too easy to guess.

LINUXspeak

passwd

Sample

Suppose that you want to change your password to sNaFfu,2, which is not a bad password. You just type passwd, press Enter, and then follow the prompts. LINUX asks for your old password and then asks you to type your new password twice. Nothing you type is displayed on-screen. It tells you if the password change succeeds.

ps — Checking up on the system

ps stands for *Process Status*. The ps command formats information in the process table so that humans can read it. Use this command (or `top`) when the system is slow or when you just want to see what is going on, such as what is running and who's on the system.

LINUXspeak

`ps [a][e][f][l][m][u]`

Argument or Option	Function
a	Shows all processes, not just those that belong to you
e	Includes environment information in output
f	Shows a family tree relationship of processes
l	Long format that includes more information about the processes
m	Displays memory usage information
u	Includes user name and start time

Sample

Your system seems slow and you wonder why. First, you can check up on what you are doing by entering the following:

`ps l`

You don't find anything that seems like a problem, so you want to see who else is running stuff and what they are doing. The following command shows you all the processes that are running on the system, who owns them, when they were started, and what sort of system resources they are using.

`ps au`

The `ps` command includes many options, including the ability to sort the output. `ps --help` lists all the choices.

su — Assuming another identity

Many people think that `su` stands for SuperUser, but it really means *Substitute User*. In other words, you can become someone else, but you need to know the password for the identity you want to assume. The command can be used to become root to do some systems administration or, if you have multiple accounts on one machine, you can become your other identity without having to log out and back in.

LINUXspeak

`su [-] [-c command] [-l] [user [args]]`

Argument or Option	Function
-	Makes the new shell act like a login shell, undoing the setting on all environment variables except TERM, HOME, and SHELL. Sets PATH to the complied-in default, changes to user's home directory, and makes the shell read its login startup file(s).
-c command	Executes command as the new user and then exits back to the user invoking su.
-l	Same as -.
user	The user ID of the identity to assume. Assumes root if not specified.
args	Any arguments, such as setting shell variables, that you want to pass to the new shell.

Logging on as root is always dangerous. If you need to run a command only occasionally as root, log on as yourself and use the -c option of su when necessary. For example, to kill a process whose number is 1234, just enter

```
su -c "kill 1234"
```

top — Monitoring system status

The top command is like an ongoing ps sorted by CPU hog factor. top runs until terminated and displays the biggest CPU hog at the top each time it repaints the screen. Some interactive commands are available after top is running. Type h to display a help list.

LINUXspeak
```
top [d delay][i][q][S][s]
```

Argument or Option	Function
d delay	Specifies the delay in seconds between screen updates. The default is five seconds.
q	Updates the display as fast as possible.
S	Includes time used by its dead child processes in a processes total.
s	Runs in secure mode, disabling nonsecure interactive commands.

w — User and system status

This command combines the type of information from ps with that from finger. It's a short-form *who is doing what* command.

LINUXspeak

w [*user*]

Argument or Option	Function
user	Only displays information for user.

## Part IV

Using X/FVWM

With LINUX, you have a choice of working in either a *command line environment* or a *graphical environment.* Because the graphical environment is more intuitive to use and allows you to display on-screen information on multiple tasks, most users prefer it over the command line environment. (However, most users keep one or more shell windows open for entering commands.)

In case your're wondering about the "alphabet soup" in the title of this part, *X* is short for *The X Window System,* a GUI (graphical user interface) environment developed at the Massachusetts Institute of Technology. It has become the de facto GUI standard for UNIX systems (and by association for LINUX as well). *FVWM* stands for *Feeble Virtual Window Manager* (the name given to it by its creator Robert Nation). FVWM has become the de facto standard for windows managers on LINUX systems.

In this part . . .

- ✔ Discovering the basics of X and window managers
- ✔ Working with FVWM and TheNextLevel
- ✔ Finding out about common GUI-based programs
- ✔ Using non-GUI programs in a GUI world
- ✔ Using shortcuts for efficient operation of your environment

An Introduction to X

The X Window System (or more commonly X) is a GUI environment available for most UNIX and UNIX-like platforms — including LINUX. X includes three pieces: the window manager, the X client, and the X server.

The Window manager

This program, as the name implies, manages windows. That is, this program gives you a method to work with the windows — to change their size, location, and things like that.

As with X servers, you have many window managers to choose from. The commercial standard is *Motif* — but the most popular window manager in the LINUX community is *FVWM*. FVWM is highly configurable (as well as free), making it a good choice.

In the past, most users configured FVWM to look like Motif, the window manager developed at the Open Software Foundation. Today, more people prefer the look of Windows 95, which is emulated by FVWM in a configuration called *FVWM95*. The default window manager for Red Hat LINUX systems is called *TheNextLevel*, a specific configuration of FVWM95. The information on programs in this chapter is independent of window managers, but any window manager functions I talk about are specific to TheNextLevel (which was developed by Greg J. Badros of Duke University).

If the look and feel of the default X environment isn't to your liking, you may want to look into other default desktops for FVWM or possibly other window managers.

The X client

The client is the program that the server works with to get your job done. The client is an applications program with the necessary hooks that enable it to communicate with an X server.

The X server

The server is the program that runs on your local computer and drives the display. This definition may sound backward in a world in which we talk about database servers and users as clients, but you can also think about it another way. The program that displays the information from the programs you are running on your screen serves you, the user.

A few more words on the X server are in order. *XFree86* is a freely available X server that comes with all LINUX distributions. Two commercial X servers are also available for LINUX: *Accelerated-X* (from Xi Graphics) and *Metro-X* (from Metro Link). XFree86 usually is adequate; but if you have a performance-critical application, a commercial alternative may be worth the cost.

The FVWM Desktop Anatomy

The LINUX desktop contains a bunch of levels, so I'll start from the top. FVWM offers multiple virtual desktops that you can select by using the *Pager.* Each desktop may be larger than the displayable screen size. This screen size is called the *virtual size* and is limited by the amount of video RAM that you have available. The screen becomes a viewpoint into the desktop. The nearby figure shows the FVWM95 Desktop on Red Hat LINUX.

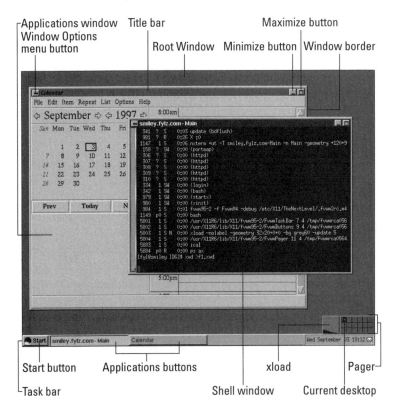

Applications windows

The following section describes how to work with an application you want to run within FVWM. These applications run in their own windows that appear as any size on a desktop. FVWM manages these windows, as well.

FVWM supplies a border for each window. You use this border to modify the characteristics of the window. The top border includes a *title bar* that displays the name of the window (which may also be the name of the application). The title bar may also contain up to ten buttons.

By default, the title bar has three buttons. Clicking the far-left task bar button displays a list of window options. Clicking on the far-right task bar button maximizes the window to fill the desktop (clicking this button a second time changes the window back to its previous size). Clicking the button to the left of the maximizing button on the title bar minimizes the window (it appears as an icon on the Task Bar).

Another characteristic of a window is that it can be *sticky,* which means that the window appears in all the desktops. The Pager is a sticky window (this feature is also commonly used for clocks and can be used for icons you want to have on all desktops).

The term *in focus* is used to describe the status of an active window. The border of the window currently in focus appears in a different color in order to identify it as the active window. The three focus methods are:

+ **Click-to-focus:** You must move the mouse into a window and click in order to bring it into focus.

+ **Focus-follows-mouse:** You only need to move the mouse to a window in order to make it active.

+ **Sloppy focus:** This focus method (available only in FVWM95) offers a combination of the other two methods. Focus follows the mouse to other windows, but if you move to the root window, the focus stays in the most recently active window.

FVWM95 also allows you to specify a focus style per window. By using this capability, you can prevent focus from automatically changing to windows where you would not typically enter data, thus removing the focus from a terminal window.

The Pager

The Pager is a module of FVWM that displays a miniature view of all the desktops. You can switch to a different desktop by clicking on that desktop's mini-image in the pager.

Directly to the left of the Pager is a rectangle that shows a jagged graph at the bottom. This graph displays the output of a program called *xload,* which shows system load over time. Essentially, the taller the graph, the greater the load.

The root window

The background (the area on the screen where no windows appear) is called the *root window*. This area normally consists of a solid color, but you can run a program that offers a changing background. Two examples are *xearth* and *xfishtank*.

The Task Bar

The Task Bar appears across the bottom of the screen. You use the Start button on the left end of the Task Bar to access menus that start additional applications. The other buttons on the Task Bar represent other programs or applications. You click these buttons to change the active (meaning, selected) task. The active task's button appears depressed; all others appear raised.

Adding Backgrounds

Backgrounds are programs that replace the boring stuff in your root window with something interesting. Three backgrounds are available in the Toys submenu of the Games pull-down menu.

Program	Function
xearth	A view of the earth from the sun. Earth rotates showing noon in the middle of the display.
xfishtank	Turns the root window into a fish tank.
xsnow	Seasonal background.

Checking Out Programs under X

A whole host of programs are designed to run under X. This section gives you a sampling of a few programs I think you will find useful. The programs include a terminal window (where you can run nongraphic applications), a viewer for PostScript files, and an appointment calendar system.

You can add any of these programs to your menus or just enter their names in a shell window to start them.

If you enter an ampersand (&) after a command name, the command starts in the background and you can continue to enter commands in that shell window.

gv — display PostScript files

The gv program is a GUI front end for GhostScript, the Postscript-to-most-anything translator. This program allows you to scale a document, print out parts of it, and otherwise manipulate a PostScript file.

Another program that acts as a front end for GhostScript is called Ghostview. It is available in the Applications pull-down menu.

ical — appointment calendar

The ical appointment calendar program allows you to do the following:

+ Schedule your day

+ Include more than one calendar file

+ Schedule reoccurring events

+ Receive alarms for upcoming events

ical stores its schedule information in a file called .calendar in your home directory.

If ical doesn't do all you need, take a look at plan. While similar to ical, plan includes the ability to schedule program executions or send you e-mail at the scheduled time of an event — and it supports long messages.

xbill — video game for LINUX

This program is a I-must-save-the-world video game. It gives you a chance to become one of those LINUX users who prevents a terrible virus from turning all the computers in the world into toasters.

xcalc — desk calculator

Xcalc is a basic calculator. You can use keystrokes to enter commands and values, use the mouse to press the calculator buttons, or a combination of the two methods. For example, to multiply 33 times 7, enter the following:

```
33*7=.
```

xeyes — watching the MouseCursor

This simple application will amuse your kids and probably amuse you, too, if you've had a very long day. MouseCursor is a pair of eyes that continually looks at the cursor.

xmag — magnifying glass

Another handy utility, xmag, allows you to magnify a portion of the screen.

1. Start xmag from a menu or by typing `xmag` at a shell prompt.

2. When the cursor changes to a corner shape, move the mouse to the upper-left corner of the area you want to magnify.

3. Click the left mouse button. You have a magnified image.

xman — display man pages

This program is a GUI front end for the `man` command. The big advantage over man is that `xman` makes searching for pages much easier. It includes documentation on itself.

xterm — terminal window

By default, an xterm is just like a *virtual console* (a text-based screen which is an alternative to running the GUI), but it appears as a window under X. The following are the advantages of an `xterm` over using multiple virtual consoles:

✦ You can display multiple xterms on the same screen (along with other X applications).

✦ You can easily cut and paste between xterms and other X applications.

✦ You can resize an xterm to the number of columns and rows you want.

✦ An xterm has a *scrollback buffer* so you can look through lines that would have scrolled off a virtual console.

If you want to know about running command-line programs under X, the best answer here is: just do it. An xterm acts just like a virtual terminal. If a program runs from the command line, it should work fine in an xterm.

Copying and pasting an xterm

You can copy text between one xterm and another or between an xterm and another application. The mouse action is shown in the following table:

Mouse Action	Function
Click and drag	Selects the text that you drag over
Double click	Selects a word
Triple click	Selects a line

To paste the text that you selected:

1. Move the mouse to the area where you want to paste a copy of the text that you selected.

2. Click the middle mouse button.

Exiting an xterm

An xterm is just like a login session. To exit an xterm, just type **exit**.

Scrolling through the xterm scrollback buffer

Each xterm maintains a buffer of previous lines that won't fit in the display window.

✦ The bar at the left shows where you are in the buffer.

✦ The length of the slider is proportional to the amount of information that fits in the window relative to the total content of the buffer.

✦ To scroll back in the buffer, click on the bar with the right mouse button.

✦ To scroll forward in the buffer, click on the bar with the left mouse button.

✦ To move the slider to a specific place in the buffer, use the center mouse button and click in the bar where you want the slider to move.

Starting an xterm

To start an xterm, do the following:

1. Click on Start.

2. Click on New shell.

An alternate way to start a new xterm is to press Ctrl+Shift+Alt+X.

xv — graphics displayer and manipulation tool

xv is a powerful tool for working with graphic images. It is best know as a viewer, but it allows conversion between formats, cropping, and modifications to images. xvscan, based on xv, includes support for HP scanners. xv is shareware.

If you had to write a book and wanted to include screen shots, you would probably want to use xwd to save the shots, but, you would need to convert them to TIF format for the publisher. xv is the ideal tool for this task.

Examining Pull-Down Menus

TheNextLevel offers a whole host of pull-down menus that you can access directly instead of having to get to them through the root (Start) menu.

Applications menu

The Applications pull-down menu offers a general assortment of applications that you can run. To access a pull-down menu and run an application:

1. Click on Start.

2. Move the mouse to the desired pull-down menu item.

3. Move the mouse to the new submenu.

4. Click on the application you wish to run.

You can press the left mouse button while the mouse cursor is over the root window to select the Start menu. You don't need to click the Start button itself. The Start menu offers access to application programs that are included with LINUX. The following applications are available in this menu:

Program Name	Function
RedBaron	Commercially licensed web browser.
Grail	Commercially licensed web browser based on Tcl/Tk and Python.
Pine	Mail user agent for sending/reading e-mail.
Emacs	An everything-including-the-kitchen-sihk-text editor.
Ghostview	GUI front end for the GhostScript PostScript interpreter (check out gv which has a nicer appearance).
XDvi	Displays .dvi (device independent) files. These files are created by various programs including the TeX and LaTeX document formatting systems.
Xview	This program is actually xv — a shareware graphics viewer and editor. If you have a scanner, an enhanced version that supports HP scanners is available at www.tummy.com.
Xedit	Simple GUI-based text editor.
GnuPlot	Plotting package from the Free Software Foundation. Type **help** in gnuplot for more information.
XFig	Basic vector graphics program.
XPaint	Basic bit-mapped drawing program.

(continued)

Program Name	Function
Xxgdb	GUI front end for gdb
gdb	GNU program debugger
XWpe	Windows Programming Environment — an integrated development environment where you can write, compile, and debug programs, including access to man page documentation
Arena Browser	Web browser from the W3 Consortium
Xlispstat	Lisp interpreter
Chipmunk Basic	BASIC interpreter
Irc	Internet Relay Chat
Minicom	Terminal emulator program similar to the DOS program Procomm
Tin	Internet news reader
Trn	Internet news reader
XGopher	Gopher client (Gopher was the online information source until the World Wide Web took over)
Xedit	A basic text editor
Xjed	Text editor written by John E. Davis

Games menu

This Games menu offers an assortment of computer games, including the following:

Program Name	Function
Arcade	Assortment of arcade games such as Tetris, Jewel, and Boing
Puzzles	Various puzzles
Toys	Fun playthings, including three window backgrounds: `xearth`, `xsnow`, and `xfishtank`
Hockeys	Assorted hockeylike games
XBoard	Chess
Spider	Solitaire-like game
XLander	Lunar lander
XPatience	Solitaire-like game
XMorph	Morphing game
XEvil	Zapping game
XBill	Watch out or your computers will become toasters (let it be a surprise!)
XGammon	Backgammon

Hosts menu

You can start terminal windows on different hosts. The listed hosts should be automatically updated if you change your network configuration. To start a terminal window on one of the listed hosts, just click on the hostname.

The last two entries (Xrsh and Rlogin) allow you start a terminal window on a remote machine. The Rlogin procedure is the one you really need to know. To perform a remote login onto any host:

1. Select Rlogin from the Hosts menu.

2. If you want to log in under a different username, click the box next to Username and enter the desired login name.

3. Click on Login.

Lock Screen menu

Lock Screen uses the same display programs as the Screensaver pull-down menu. The difference is that you cannot just press a key to get your X session back. To unlock your screen:

1. Press Enter.

2. Type your password and press Enter.

Multimedia menu

This Multimedia menu offers access to the LINUX programs that work with sound and video.

Program Name	Function
XMixer	Controls your sound card volume settings
XPlayCd	Plays audio CDs
Tracker	Works with .mod files
Playmidi	Plays a MIDI file
Xmplay	Plays an MPEG file

Preferences menu

This menu allows you to modify the characteristics of your window manager.

Program Name	Function
FvwmConfig	Modifies your FVWM configuration
Root Cursor	Changes the appearance of the cursor in the root window
Mouse	Changes the speed and the left- or right-hand setting of the mouse
Colors	Modifies your color map
Audio	Turns audio on or off
Scroll Setup	Establishes the conditions by which a new desktop is displayed when the cursor is moved to the edge of the current desktop
X Resources	Modifies your .Xdefaults and .Xresources files
Save Desktop to new.xinitrc	Saves the changes you make to the desktop

Screensaver menu

The Screensaver pull-down menu allows you to select a screensaver program to run when the computer is idle. To exit the screensaver, press any key on the keyboard (shift is a good, harmless choice). (The list of screensaver submenus is fairly lengthy, and you can have some fun discovering them on your own.)

System Utilities menu

The systems utilities listed here are more hardcore techno-nerd items than those that appear in the Utilities menu. You use them to get information about or to modify system features. (The truth is, many of these utilities aren't absolutely necessary because they are part of the default environment of TheNextLevel.)

Program Name	Function
Root shell	Starts a shell as root
Msgs	Brings up a console window so you can see messages that are being logged to the console
Top	Starts the top program to show system/program status
Identify Window	Displays information about a selected window
Window Info	Displays information about a selected window
Talk Module	Command line interface to active copy of FVWM
Pager Module	Starts the Pager
Task Bar	Starts the Task Bar
Fvwm Command	Sends a command to FVWM
Reread .Xdefaults	Reads .Xdefaults into active window manager

Program Name	Function
Restart Fvwm2	Reinitializes FVWM
Refresh Screen	Redraws the screen
Recapture All Windows	FVWM connects to all X clients

Utilities menu

Utilities are essentially programs to perform system tasks. The following menu lists the utility program choices:

Program Name	Function
Control Panel	Red Hat systems administration control panel.
Glint	GUI-based Red Hat package installer.
Color XTerm	Starts another terminal window.
Manual Pages	Runs xman to view online man pages.
XCalc	Desk calculator.
Calendar	Runs the ical appointment calendar program.
Xfm	GUI desktop/file manager. This utility is really an alternative to the pull-down menu system that I describe this section.
Magnifying glass	Starts xmag, which shows an enlarged display of a portion of the screen.
Xload	Shows system load (average number of tasks waiting to run). This utility runs as part of the standard desktop.
Fontsel	Selects a display font.
Editres	Edits the X Resources of an X client.
Clipboard	Displays the clipboard as saved by an X client.
XOsview	Displays system load, CPU, memory and swap usage, net traffic and interrupts.
Clock	Analog clock.
XBiff	New mail arrival warning utility.
Xev	Prints contents of X events.

Window Operations menu

The Windows Operations pull-down menu contains options that direct the window manager to take some action on a client window. I describe most of these actions elsewhere in this part, so this section simply lists them.

You can select the Window Operations pull-down menu by clicking and holding the center mouse button while the mouse cursor is on the title bar.

Program Name	Function
Move	Moves a window by using click and drag
Resize	Changes the size of a window using click and drag
Raise	Moves window to the top of any stacked windows
Lower	Moves window to the bottom, underneath other stacked windows
Hide/Restore	Iconifies a window
Maximize/Reset	Maximizes a window or sets it back to its premaximized size
Maximize Tall/Reset	Maximizes the height of a window or sets it back to its premaximized size
Maximize Wide/Reset	Maximizes the width of a window or sets it back to its premaximized size
Delete	Deletes a window
Close	Nicely terminates the application running a window or running in a terminal window
Kill	Kills the application running a window (not so nicely)
ScrollBar	Add scroll bars to a window
Capture Windows	Runs xwd to capture a window
Window List Module	Displays a list of modules (the same information that is displayed in the task bar)
Switch to	Changes the active window
Refresh Screen	Redraws the screen

Exiting X

If you are running a GUI-only system, this sequence logs you out. Otherwise, you need to type **exit** at the shell prompt after you get out of X.

1. Move to the root window.

2. Click the left mouse button.

3. Select Exit Fvwm.

4. Select Yes, Really Quit from the submenu.

TIP

The key combination to make an emergency exit from X is Ctrl+Alt+Backspace. This key sequence exits X without letting any of your applications clean up. You can disable this key combination in your X configuration file /etc/X11/XF86Config.

Modifying Window Characteristics

Clicking on the left-most button in a window's title bar activates a pull-down menu, where you can modify the characteristics of the window.

Closing a window

Closing is a graceful way to ask the X client to disappear (as opposed to when you kill a window and the program relinquishes control of the window). To close a window, do the following:

1. Click on the left-most button in the title bar.

2. Click on Close from the pull-down menu that appears.

Destroying a window

The distinction between Close and Destroy is that the Close command is "friendly" — it asks the client program to remove itself. If, however, the window does not understand the message or you elect to use Kill from the pull-down menu, the window is destroyed by the window manager. Because this can cause the application to crash and burn, you resort to the Kill option only if the window has not responded to the Close request. Here's what you do in that case:

1. Click on the left-most button in the title bar.

2. Click on Kill.

Maximizing a window

Maximizing a window expands it to fit on the screen.

1. Click on the left-most button in the title bar.

2. Click on Maximize from the pull-down menu that appears.

Minimizing a window

The fancy word for minimizing a window is *iconification,* which means replacing the window with an icon. To iconify a window:

1. Click on the left-most button in the title bar.

2. Click on Minimize.

When you iconify a window under FVWM95, the window itself disappears, but the entry on the Task Bar remains. To restore the window, click the icon on the Task Bar.

Moving a window

You may want to move a window on your desktop so you can display another window or as part of a general desktop cleanup. You can do this:

1. Click on the left-most button in the title bar.

2. Click on Move. The mouse cursor turns into a four-headed arrow.

3. Move the mouse and the window follows.

4. When you are happy with the new window position, click again.

TIP

An easier way to move a window is to click on the title bar (where no button appears) and then drag the window to its new location. The window stays where it is when you release the mouse button.

Resizing a window

There are lots of ways to change the size of a window. These include making it zero size (kill), maximization, and anything in between.

The most common way to modify window size is to do the following:

1. Move the mouse to one of the corners of the window. The mouse cursor changes into an L-shaped icon with an arrow pointing to the intersection of the two lines.

2. Click on the corner of the window and drag in or out to adjust its size.

3. When you are satisfied with the window size, release the mouse button.

An alternate method is:

1. Click on the left-most button in the title bar.

2. Click on Size.

3. Move the mouse to any corner of the window. A shadow of the window border appears.

4. Move the mouse until the window is the size desired.

5. Click to set the new size.

Sticking/unsticking a window

A *sticky* window appears on all the desktops (just like the Pager does). While this function doesn't appear in the Window Characteristics menu, it is available by other means. The sticky window characteristic toggles — select it once, and the window becomes sticky; select it again, and the window becomes unsticky. To toggle stickiness:

1. Select the window.

2. Enter Ctrl+Shift+Alt+S.

Mousing with X

You can use X without a mouse, but it isn't very likely you will want to do so. Here are some basic rules to get you up to speed on using the mouse:

✦ Most serious mouse work is done with the left mouse button, which you use to pull down menus, select programs, and perform other operations.

✦ You generally use the right mouse button within applications or menus for contextual information.

✦ You can cut text from a text window by highlighting it with the left mouse button.

✦ You can paste selected text with the center mouse button. (In some window managers or X configurations, this function only works when you press the Shift key.)

If you have a two-button mouse (or if your three-button mouse isn't configured correctly), you can configure X so that pressing the left and right buttons together is the equivalent of pressing the middle button. Every install GUI and text mode for each distribution has a different way of dealing with this. *See* the comments in the distribution's file /etc/X11/XF86Config for details.

When in the root window, each mouse button has a defined function:

Button	Function
Left	Activates the Start menu
Center	Displays active window list
Right	Activates the Applications Button Bar

When the mouse cursor is positioned over a window title bar, the mouse buttons have another set of functions:

Button	Function
Left	Raises window on top of other windows
Left and drag	Resizes window
Center	Activates the Window Ops menu
Right	Raises or hides the window (this is a toggle)

Moving around the Screen

You can move the mouse cursor around the desktop without using the mouse. (Coarse cursor movements are quick; fine movements are slower.) The following table shows the key sequences for doing so.

Key Sequence	Function
Ctrl+Shift+Alt+H	Coarse cursor left
Ctrl+Shift+Alt+J	Coarse cursor down
Ctrl+Shift+Alt+K	Coarse cursor up
Ctrl+Shift+Alt+L	Coarse cursor right
Ctrl+Shift+Alt+Y	Fine cursor left
Ctrl+Shift+Alt+U	Fine cursor down
Ctrl+Shift+Alt+I	Fine cursor up
Ctrl+Shift+Alt+O	Fine cursor right

Starting Applications

LINUX offers two ways to start applications: from a shell window (xterm) or from a menu. Typically, you put the programs that you use regularly in the menus. After all, that's what a GUI is for. If the program you want to run is not in a menu or if you want to start it with different arguments or options, you can do so from an xterm. If you append an ampersand (&) to the command line, the application starts in the background (which means that your shell window will be available for other functions).

Starting X

If your login screen is graphical, your system is probably running xdm, and you are always in X. If, on the other hand, you have a text-mode login, you will have to start X yourself.

1. Enter your login name and password to log in.

2. Type `startx` and press Enter to start X.

A default screen appears, displaying the Pager and the Task Bar. If you are running the default Red Hat configuration, a single terminal window, called an xterm, also comes up.

Most distributions offer a GUI environment at one run level, a command line environment at another run level. Most likely, you can change the default run level in /etc/inittab to select whether your system comes up in GUI or command line mode.

Switching Tasks

You can switch between tasks using multiple methods. If the task you want to switch to is visible, you can just click on its window. Otherwise, just click on its entry in the Task Bar. A third method of switching tasks is:

1. Click the center mouse button to get the active task pull-down menu.

2. Click on the desired task.

Using Button Bars

Button bars allow you to access an action directly without going to a menu. You can display most of the pull-down menus described in the following sections as button bars. If you can select the title line by clicking it, you can create a button bar that offers those menu options. To bring up a button bar:

1. Click on the Start button.

2. Move the mouse to the desired submenu.

3. Click on the submenu title.

The button bar appears in some free real estate at the top of your screen.

One of the handiest submenus to turn into a button bar is the Window Operations submenu. You can then modify any window (or even a button bar) by just clicking on the button, moving the mouse cursor to the window where you want to perform the operation, and clicking.

Using Keyboard Shortcuts

For people who are allergic to a mouse (take me, for example), you can generally find another way to talk to the window manager. The following key combinations are the default shortcuts for Red Hat LINUX. The shortcuts work in the root window and in any other window that doesn't capture and use the key sequences for something else.

Key Sequence	Function
Ctrl+Shift+F1	Displays a pop-up Window Operations menu
Ctrl+Shift+F2	Displays a pop-up task list
Ctrl+Shift+F3	Displays a pop-up Hosts submenu
Ctrl+Shift+F4	Displays a pop-up Applications submenu
Ctrl+Shift+F5	Displays a pop-up Utilities submenu
Ctrl+Shift+F6	Displays a pop-up Multimedia submenu
Ctrl+Shift+F7	Moves window
Ctrl+Shift+F8	Resizes window
Ctrl+Alt+F1	Selects first *virtual console* (a text-based screen)
Ctrl+Alt+F2	Selects second virtual console
Ctrl+Alt+F3	Selects third virtual console
Ctrl+Alt+F4	Selects fourth virtual console
Ctrl+Alt+F5	Selects fifth virtual console
Ctrl+Alt+F6	Selects sixth virtual console
Ctrl+Alt+F7	Selects seventh virtual console (this is the X graphics console)
Ctrl+Alt+F8	Selects eighth virtual console
Ctrl+Shift+Alt+P	Displays a pop-up Preferences menu
Ctrl+Shift+Alt+R	Refreshes the screen
Ctrl+Shift+Alt+W	Displays a pop-up Window Operations menu
Ctrl+Shift+Alt+X	Starts a new xterm (terminal window)
Ctrl+Shift+Alt+Z	Displays a pop-up root menu
Alt+Tab	Toggles between the two most-recently active windows

When you are within a menu, you can select a menu item by pressing the key that corresponds to the underlined letter in the item you want to select.

## Part V

Text Editors and Working with Text

You use text editors to write and edit messages and other text files. Text editors, however, are not word processors. They allow you to edit text files, but they do not offer sophisticated commands to format text. If you need such formatting, you either can look for a WYSIWYG word processor such as Applixware or StarOffice or use a text formatter such as LaTeX or groff, both of which are included with your LINUX system.

In this part . . .

- ✔ Using Pico or joe to work with text
- ✔ Editing (the industrial-strength kind) with vi and Emacs
- ✔ Formatting text with fmt and groff
- ✔ Checking your spelling with ispell

Choosing an Editor

Some folks would sooner fight to the death than switch text editors. If you already have a favorite editor, then just stick with it. But if you are shopping for an editor, here's some advice.

✦ If you are a beginner, take a serious look at joe. It is very powerful and has on-screen help and many modes to humor most users.

✦ Pico, as popular as it is, offers nothing that joe doesn't already have. It is the default editor for pine so many people are using pico without even realizing that they are.

✦ If you expect to do a large volume of editing — that is, hours per day — you need vi or Emacs.

✦ vi integrates the best with other UNIX/LINUX tools. It uses many of the same capabilities as those tools and generally acts more like a UNIX-type command than the other editors do. For example, Regular Expressions in vi work just like they do in awk, sed, and grep.

✦ Emacs is its own environment — many Emacs users just live in Emacs all day.

✦ Some people are frustrated by the two modes of vi — one to enter text, one to edit text. However, you can generally do more work with less keystrokes in vi than with other editors.

✦ On a system with limited resources, vi is the best choice because it is much smaller than Emacs.

In this part, I first mention two editors with training wheels: joe and Pico. I then present two industrial-strength editors: vi and Emacs. If none of these tools meets your fancy, keep shopping. You have many more LINUX editors to choose from.

Editing Text with joe

joe (Joe's Own Editor) is a simple-to-use text editor (written by one Joseph H. Allen) that offers reasonably good capabilities. joe is the chameleon of editors and is willing to pretend it is another editor if you ask it nicely. You do so by calling joe by a different name. Here's how that works: Within Linux, there are links (different names for the same file) that all point to the same program. When joe starts up, it checks to see what name you used to invoke it and, based on that information, determines its mode of operation.

Checking out joe commands

joe is a non-moded editor, which means that joe enters what you type into the file. You use control characters to issue commands. This is distinct from vi in which you use one mode to enter text and another mode to edit text.

joe has a large command set — all of which are covered in the help screens. The table below lists just some basic commands:

Command	What It Does
Backspace	Deletes the character to the left of the cursor
Enter	Inserts a line break
Tab	Inserts a tab character
@da	Moves the cursor up one line
@ua	Moves the cursor down one line
@ra	Moves the cursor right one character
@la	Moves the cursor left one character
Ctrl+A	Moves the cursor to the beginning of the line
Ctrl+B	Moves back one character
Ctrl+C	Exits without saving changes
Ctrl+D	Deletes character under the cursor (or line-break if the cursor is at the end of the line)
Ctrl+E	Moves the cursor to the end of the line
Ctrl+F	Moves forwards one character
Ctrl+J	Deletes from the cursor to the end of the line
Ctrl+K+A	Centers a line within the margins
Ctrl+K+D	Saves the current file
Ctrl+K+E	Edits a different file
Ctrl+K+J	Reformats the paragraph cursor is in
Ctrl+K+R	Inserts a file into the current edit session
Ctrl+K+U	Moves the cursor to the beginning of the file
Ctrl+K+V	Moves the cursor to the end of the file
Ctrl+N	Moves to the next line
Ctrl+P	Moves to the preceding line
Ctrl+R	Refreshes the screen
Ctrl+T+L	Sets left margin
Ctrl+T+R	Sets right margin
Ctrl+T+T	Toggles overtype mode

(continued)

Command	What It Does
Ctrl+T+W	Toggles word wrap (normally on for text files, off for program files)
Ctrl+U	Scrolls the cursor up half a screen
Ctrl+V	Scrolls the cursor down half a screen
Ctrl+Y	Deletes the entire line cursor is on
Ctrl+_	Undoes last command
Ctrl+ ^	Undoes the last undo

Exiting joe

To exit joe, follow these steps:

1. Press Ctrl+K+X.

2. If joe asks you whether you want to save changes made to the file, press y to save and n to exit without saving.

If you changed the file, joe prompts you for a filename.

Getting help

joe is so friendly because it offers on-screen help. For example

✦ Press Ctrl+K+H to bring up the first help screen. It appears on the top half of the screen.

✦ Press Ctrl+K+H again to dismiss the help screen.

✦ While help is on-screen, you can page through it by pressing Esc followed by a comma or Esc followed by a period.

Another source of help is the *man page* (or LINUX manual page). The man page contains many command line options that change the operation of joe.

Searching for text

You can search for and replace text using joe's search mode.

To enter search mode, follow these steps:

1. Press Ctrl+K+F.

2. Enter the text to search for and press Enter. joe asks you to choose an option.

3. Press Enter to start a forward search or use any of the following options:

Command	What It Does
b	Searches backward instead of forward
i	Ignores case differences when matching
nnn	Searches for the occurrence *nnn* of the search text
r	Replaces text (see the next table)

If you choose to replace text, you have your choice of the following commands:

Command	What It Does
y	Replaces the text and continues the search
n	Does not replace the text and continues the search
r	Replaces all remaining occurrences of the text
Ctrl+C	Cancels the search

If you want to repeat a search with the same search string, it is not necessary to reenter the string. All you have to do is press Ctrl+L to repeat the previous search.

Starting joe

To start joe with its native "personality," enter joe followed by a filename. If you elect to start joe as something else, use the following names:

Command	Function
joe	Executes joe with its native personality
jstar	Executes joe as WordStar
jmacs	Executes joe as Emacs
jPico	Executes joe as Pico
rjoe	Restricts joe — you can only edit files specified on the command line

What else joe does

joe can do many, many more wonderful things. Here are a few of them:

- ✦ Work with Regular Expressions
- ✦ Move, copy, save, or delete blocks of text
- ✦ Auto-indent blocks of text
- ✦ Edit in multiple windows
- ✦ Define and use macros

Editing Text with Pico

Pico is a simple editor for doing simple things with your text files. It was derived from *MicroEmacs 3.6* by Dave G. Conroy and copyrighted by the University of Washington. If you prefer complexity on the level of astro science, use vi. If you want to use a steamshovel to eat a candy bar, use Emacs. However, if you just want to do some basic editing to a file, choose Pico.

Checking out Pico commands

The following is a comprehensive list of Pico commands all of which are control sequences.

Command	What It Does
Ctrl+A	Moves the cursor to the beginning of the line
Ctrl+B	Moves the cursor backward one character
Ctrl+C	Displays file statistics
Ctrl+D	Deletes the character under the cursor
Ctrl+E	Moves the cursor to the end of the line
Ctrl+F	Moves the cursor forward one character
Ctrl+G	Displays the help screen
Ctrl+J	Justifies the current paragraph
Ctrl+K	Cuts out the current line of text
Ctrl+L	Refreshes the display
Ctrl+N	Moves the cursor down one line
Ctrl+O	Saves the file
Ctrl+P	Moves the cursor up one line
Ctrl+R	Reads a file into the current editor file
Ctrl+T	Spell checks the document
Ctrl+U	Pastes cut text
Ctrl+V	Moves the cursor forward one page of text
Ctrl+W	Searches for text within the file
Ctrl+X	Exits Pico
Ctrl+Y	Moves the cursor backward one page of text

Exiting Pico

If you realize that Pico is not the place you want to be, or that you've opened the wrong file, you can exit Pico by following these steps:

1. Press Ctrl+X.

2. If Pico asks you whether you wish to save changes made to the file, press Y to save and N to exit without saving.

Importing a file into an edit session

To insert a file into the file you are currently editing, follow these steps:

1. Position your cursor to the location where you want to insert the file.

2. Press Ctrl+R. Pico asks you to enter the name of file that you want to insert.

3. Enter the filename (including its directory if you are in a different directory) that you want to insert and then press Enter. If you're not sure what the file is called or where it is located, press Ctrl+T. Pico looks around for the file.

4. Once you have your filename highlighted, press Enter, and the file drops into your current document at the current cursor position.

Maneuvering around a file

Maneuvering in Pico is rather straightforward. The up arrow moves you up, the down arrow moves you down, the left arrow moves you left, and you can guess the rest.

For more complicated file maneuvering, use Ctrl+Y to move up a page and Ctrl+V to move down a page. If you forget these commands, just look at the command menu at the bottom of the screen.

Starting Pico

Whether you want to use Pico to edit an existing file or to create a new file, type Pico followed by the filename you want to create or edit to start Pico.

In Pico, you need to remember only two things:

✦ Pressing Ctrl+X gets you out of whatever you get into.

✦ All the common commands are listed on the menu at the bottom of the screen. When in doubt, refer to the command menu. If you are still in doubt, press Ctrl+G to view the built-in documentation.

Editing Text with Emacs

The big daddy of all editors, Emacs Editing Macros, was written and is still maintained by Richard M. Stallman. I tell you only how to start it and how to get out of it (something I feel is less than intuitive), and I provide a list of common commands.

Why is the E in Emacs capitalized? After all, you must enter the program name (emacs) in all lowercase letters when you want to start it. However, people in the know always capitalize the E when referring to Emacs. Go figure.

Checking out Emacs commands

Unlike vi, Emacs is not moded. That means you can type a command at any time. However, you sometimes have to use some strange combination of key sequences to perform certain commands.

The arrow, PageUp, PageDown, Home, and End keys do what you would expect. Thus, you can use them rather than the control key sequences.

Emacs has always used two keys for commands — Ctrl and Meta. Most keyboards don't have a Meta key. If your keyboard has an Alt key, use it instead of the Meta key. If your keyboard doesn't have an Alt key, use Esc.

Command	What It Does
Meta+<	Moves the cursor to the beginning of the file.
Meta+>	Moves the cursor to the end of the file.
Meta+%	Replaces all occurrences of one piece of text with another. Emacs asks you for the text you want to replace with the text you want to replace it with.
Ctrl+@	Puts a mark at the cursor location. After you move the cursor, you can move or copy the text between the mark and the cursor by using Ctrl+W or Meta+W.
Ctrl+A	Moves the cursor to the beginning of the line.
Ctrl+B	Moves the cursor back one character.
Meta+B	Moves the cursor back one word.
Ctrl+D	Deletes the character under the cursor.
Meta+D	Deletes the current word.
Ctrl+E	Moves the cursor to the end of the line.
Ctrl+F	Moves the cursor forward one character.
Meta+F	Moves the cursor forward one word.
Ctrl+G	Cancels the current command.

Command	What It Does
Ctrl+H	Enters the online help system.
Ctrl+H+C	Displays the command that runs when you press a particular key.
Ctrl+H+T	Runs a tutorial about Emacs.
Ctrl+K	Deletes ("kills") the text from the cursor to the end of the line and stores it in the kill buffer.
Ctrl+N	Moves the cursor to the next line.
Ctrl+P	Moves the cursor to the preceding line.
Meta+Q	Reformats the current paragraph, using word wrap, so that the lines are full.
Ctrl+S	Searches for text. When you find what you are looking for, press Esc or move the cursor. To repeat the search, press Ctrl+S again.
Ctrl+T	Transposes the character before the cursor with the one under the cursor.
Meta+T	Transposes the word under the cursor with the following word.
Meta+U	Capitalizes all letters of the current word.
Ctrl+V	Scrolls down one screen.
Meta+V	Scrolls up one screen.
Ctrl+W	Deletes ("whomps") the text between the mark (set by using Ctrl+@) and the cursor, and stores the text in the kill buffer. To get it back, press Ctrl+Y.
Meta+W	Copies the text between the mark and the cursor to the kill buffer so that you can insert copies of it by entering Ctrl+Y.
Ctrl+X, Ctrl+C	Exits Emacs.
Ctrl+X, Ctrl+S	Saves the file.
Ctrl+X, U	Undoes the last change.
Meta+X doctor	Stops doing useful work and starts *doctor mode,* playing a game in which Emacs responds to your statements with questions. Save your work first. Not all versions of Emacs support this mode.
Ctrl+Y	Inserts ("yanks") the text that is in the kill buffer and places it after the cursor.
Del (Delete key)	Deletes the character under the cursor.

Exiting Emacs

To exit Emacs, simply follow these steps:

1. Press Ctrl+X, Ctrl+S to save your work.

2. Press Ctrl+X, Ctrl+C to exit to the shell.

Starting Emacs

Just type `emacs` to get started. If you want to create a new file or edit an existing file, type

`emacs` *file*

Emacs starts up and displays the file starting at the beginning.

Editing Text with vi

vi (which stands for *visual editor,* originally written by Bill Joy) is really just a VIsual front end on top of the capabilities of ed, a line editor. Most people have a hate-love relationship with vi. They realize that vi helps them edit faster than ever before. So even though vi can be maddeningly complex, users can't help loving it.

Defining vi modes

vi is a *moded editor.* This means that when you are in command mode, all the standard keyboard keys perform editing functions. You can always press Esc to get into command mode. If you are already in command mode when you press Esc, vi beeps, but no harm is done.

This idea of moded editors used to be very popular but the introduction of WYSIWYG word processors has made the use of modes almost nonexistent. (First, I'll attempt to clear up any confusion about modes before we get into the details of vi.)

Modes can increase your efficiency. If you do a lot of work before changing modes then you can decrease the number of keystrokes you need to enter to accomplish a task.

vi offers two modes — one to enter text and one to edit text. These modes are called *input mode* and *command mode.*

+ When you type something in input mode that entry is inserted into the file you are editing. A host of commands can get you into input mode, i being the most popular.

+ When you type something in command mode it is interpreted as a command to vi. One command, Esc, gets you into command mode.

Deleting text

To delete text, simply follow these steps:

1. Move the cursor to the character that you want to delete.

2. Press **x**.

vi deletes the character and moves the remainder of the line to the left.

To delete a line, move the cursor to it and type dd.

If you want to replace a single character, you don't have to delete it and then insert its replacement. Simply press r followed by the replacement character.

Exiting vi

Follow these steps to exit vi:

1. Press Esc to get into or make sure you are in command mode.

2. Type ZZ to exit and return to the shell prompt.

vi saves your file if you have modified it, before exiting.

It is common practice for users to exit vi by typing :wq followed by Enter. There are two things wrong with this. One is that the w tells vi to unconditionally write the file. This means that the last modify date that the system maintains is updated, even if there were no changes to the file. On the other hand, ZZ writes the file only if it has been modified. The second thing wrong with this exit technique is that you should never use four keystrokes when three will do.

If you don't want to save your changes, type :q! and press Enter. vi exits without making the changes to your file.

If you want to save without exiting the editor, type :w and pressing Enter. vi saves your current file at this point and allows you to continue editing.

Inserting text from other places

Why invent text when you already have what you need somewhere else? Sometimes the best source of text is from another file or from the output of a command. vi makes it easy to include either source into the file you are editing.

✦ If you want to read another file into your current editing session, just type :r filename and press Enter. The file will be read in at the current cursor location.

✦ Ever wonder how people who write books on LINUX manage to include all the examples of command output? You can include the output of a command in your current editing session by typing :r !command and pressing Enter.

Recovering from a mistake

Don't panic if you make a typo and part of your file vanishes. Just press u, and vi undoes your last change. And, of course, if you then decide that you don't really want to undo your last change, just press u again, and vi undoes what it just did.

If you have been editing on one line and decide you want to start over, type **U**. vi undoes all of your changes on that line (since you got there).

Repeating commands

To repeat commands, follow these steps:

1. Enter the number of times you want the command repeated.

2. Enter the command.

For example, to delete ten words, type 10dw.

When you enter 10dw, you really tell vi to delete one word ten times. You can also say d10w, which tells vi to delete ten words once. You can delete two words five times with 5d2w. Yes, this works.

Assume you have a document in which you want to change some but not all of the occurrences of fly to drive, you can combine the n and . (dot) commands. (The dot command repeats the last replacement command.) First, search for fly using the / command. Then use n to search again. Once you have found an occurrence you want to change, use the cw command to make the change. You can now use n and . to continue your seek-and-destroy mission.

Replacing text

Follow these steps to replace text:

1. Enter : to get into ed command mode.

2. Enter a range you want the command applied to (if you don't enter a range then the command is applied to the current line only).

3. Press s, the search command, followed by /.

4. Enter the text you want to replace followed by /.

5. Enter the replacement text followed by /.

6. Enter any options you want applied to the command.

7. Press Enter to execute the command.

You can use many forms of these replace commands; each allows you to specify line ranges or search patterns. The most basic substitute command consists of something like the following line

`:rangess/old_pattern/new_text/options`

followed by Enter.

In this example, `range` specifies the lines to apply the command to (the current line is the default); `old_pattern` is a Regular Expression to match the text to be replaced; `new_text` is the replacement text and `options` affect how the command operates. The g option is global — it changes every occurrence of `old_pattern` that matches the text being replaced (the default is limited to only the first match in each line). The c option asks to confirm the change — it displays the pending change and ask for confirmation before making it.

To exchange the position of two letters, move the cursor to the first letter and enter xp. The x deletes the letter under the cursor, and the p puts it back after the next letter. If you frequently transpose letters (for example, I tend to type *teh* for *the*), you can set up an abbreviation so vi automatically corrects your mistake when you first type it. If, for example, you use the command :ab teh the followed by Enter, vi *automatically* changes *teh* to *the*.

You specify line ranges using the format `first,last`. You can use numbers, or you can use . (dot) as shorthand for the current line and $ as shorthand for the last line. For example, 5,10 refers to lines five through ten and 1,. refers to all lines up to and including the current line.

The ultimate shorthand for line ranges is %, which you can use to represent all lines in the file. It's equivalent to 1,$.

To change the case of the letter under the cursor, just enter ~. You can precede ~ with a number to change the case of more than one letter.

Sample

Suppose that you receive an e-mail message that contains some good jokes about Microsoft that has been forwarded so many times that most of the lines start with > >. You can enter the following command to clean up the file:

`:%s/^> >//`

Then press Enter. This command replaces (indicated by the %) > > at the beginning of every line (indicated by the ^) with nothing (the lack of any text between the second and third slash).

Saving vi settings

If you have a set of options, key maps, and abbreviations that you always want to use with vi, you can save them in your .exrc file by following these steps:

1. Edit the .exrc file in your home directory.

2. Enter the desired commands into the file.

3. Save the file.

vi reads the .exrc file every time it starts, so you have these settings available each time you start vi. This is the ideal place to put commands such as abbreviations and settings that you want to establish as your default.

The following example .exrc file sets the right margin to eight characters, sets a spelling correction abbreviation for teh, and, well, sets another interesting abbreviation. (You can't blame a guy for trying.) Note that the : is optional at the beginning of commands when they are placed in this file.

```
+——————————————+
|:set wrapmargin=8 |
|:ab teh the |
|:ab Win95 LINUX |
|~ |
|~ |
|~ |
|.exrc: unmodified: line 1. |
+——————————————————+
```

Searching for text

If you want to search for some text, follow these steps:

1. Press / to get into search mode.

2. Type the text you want to search for.

3. Press Enter.

The easiest way to find something in a file is to search for it. The / command searches forward for the pattern (actually, the Regular Expression) that you enter after it. The ? command searches in the reverse direction.

Press n to repeat the last search from the current cursor location. You can also repeat the last search in the opposite direction by pressing N.

Sample

The following figure gives you a "window" into a file and shows you the positions of the cursor about to be described.

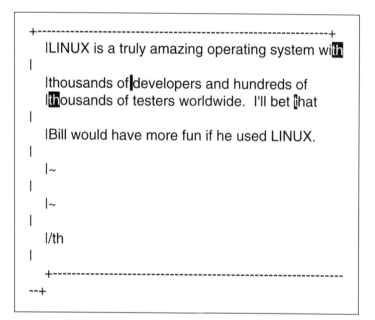

Assume the cursor is initially positioned at the beginning of the word developers. When you enter /, the cursor then moves down to the status line. After entering a search string (th) and pressing enter, the cursor moves forward to the next occurrence of thousands. Press n to repeat the search and the cursor moves to the t in that. There are no more forward-direction occurrences of th in the file, so the search wraps around to the beginning. Press n again and the cursor moves to the th at the end of the word with on the first line.

Setting options

Editing options can be divided into two types: those that are on or off, and those that have a value assigned to them. You can configure these options in many different ways.

✦ To set an on/off option to on, type :set *option_name* and press Enter.

✦ To set an on/off option to off, type :set no*option_name* and press Enter.

✦ To assign a value to an option, type `:set` option_*name*=*value*.

Here are some of the more common editing options:

Option	Type	What It Does
number	on/off	Displays line numbers
shiftwidth	value (8 default)	Determines the number of columns the shift commands move a line
showmatch	on/off	Displays matching parenthesis, brackets, and braces
showmode	on/off	Displays the current vi mode in the lower right of the screen
tabstop	value (8 default)	Determines number of characters between tabs
wrapmargin	value (off)	Determines number of character spaces to allow for the right margin

To display your current option setting, type `:set all` and press Enter.

Starting vi

To start vi, type `vi` *filename* at the shell prompt.

If the file does not exist, vi creates it. vi then displays a window into the file. If the file is not large enough to fill all the lines of the screen, empty lines appear as tildes (~). The filename appears on the last line of the screen (called the *status line*). You are now in command mode.

To enter vi and have the window display at a particular location in a file, enter `vi +/pattern filename` (with *pattern* and *filename* replaced with the actual commands) at the shell prompt. vi starts with the cursor located on the first occurrence of pattern. Note that this pattern is actually a Regular Expression (*see* Part X).

Using Input mode

You enter text in input mode. Some people call it insert mode, so don't be confused if I also call it insert mode. No matter what you call it, you enter text by following these steps.

1. Press i (for insert).

2. Type your text, pressing Enter where you want to break the lines.

3. When you are done inputting, type Esc to return to command mode.

You can enter insert mode in other ways. You can determine where the text will be inserted by using different commands, as the following table shows.

Command	Action	Result
i	insert	Inserts text at the current cursor location
I	insert	Inserts text at the beginning of the current line
o	open	Inserts a new line below the current line
O	open	Inserts a new line above the current line
a	append	Inserts text after the current cursor location
A	append	Inserts text after the last character in the current line

When entering text you sometimes need to insert a character, such as Esc or Enter, that has a special meaning to vi. To turn off this special meaning, press Ctrl+V before the desired character. For example, to enter an Esc character while in insert mode, press Ctrl+V, Esc.

vi includes two features to help you make sure your parentheses, brackets, and braces match. If you set the showmatch option (*see* the section "Setting options" later in this part of the book), the cursor flashes back to the matching parenthesis, bracket, or brace when you enter the closing one.

In command mode, if you press % while the cursor is on a parenthesis, bracket, or brace, the cursor moves to its mate.

Using operators and objects

You can use vi much more efficiently if you work on objects (such as words or lines) rather than a single character at a time. Many vi commands consist of an operator — what action to take — and an object — what to apply the action to.

Operator	What It Means
c	change
d	delete
y	yank (copy to an internal buffer)

Object	What It Means
^	beginning of line
$	end of line

(continued)

Object	What It Means
w	one word forward
W	one word forward including punctuation
b	one word back
B	one word back including punctuation
e	end of current word
E	end of current word including punctuation
)	next sentence
(	previous sentence
j	forward one line
k	back one line
h	left one character
l	right one character

Assume the cursor is on the first t in testers in the example shown in the section "Searching for text" earlier in this part. Some commands and their results follow:

Command	Result
2dw	Two words (testers worldwide) are deleted.
2dW	Two words and the following period and space (testers worldwide.) are deleted.
d^	The two words at the beginning of the line and the space after them (thousands of) are deleted.
d)	The remainder of the sentence (testers worldwide.) is deleted.

If you use an object alone (without an operator), vi moves the cursor the specified distance but doesn't modify the file.

Sample

Armed with operators and objects, you can make some simple changes. Using the figure on the following page, if you want to replace the word at the current cursor location (snerd) with framastat, place the cursor on the first character of snerd, type cwframastat and press Esc.

Wrapping lines

vi automatically breaks lines for you if you tell it how much space you want it to allow for the right margin. Use the :set wrapmargin command to do this. For example, to allow a ten-character right margin type :set wrapmargin=10 followed by Enter.

```
    +---------------------------------------------------------------
--+
    |I really like working with my █nerd.  It
|
    |is a very cool device.
|
    |~
|
    |~
|
    |~
|
    |
|
    +---------------------------------------------------------------
--+
```

cursor shown on the last t in framastat]

```
    +---------------------------------------------------------------
--+
    |I really like working with my framastat█. It
|
    |is a very cool device.
|
    |~
|
    |~
|
    |~
|
    |
|
    +---------------------------------------------------------------
--+
```

You can precede many vi commands with a *repeat count.* This is a matter of entering a number to get the command to execute multiple times. But be careful: If you accidentally type a number before entering insert mode, for example, vi inserts that number when you exit to command mode. Before you panic, check out "Recovering from a mistake" earlier in this part.

This is just a sampling of what vi can do. A list of every vi command would fill a couple dozen pages of this book. A handy vi reference card is available from SSC at www.ssc.com.

Formatting Text with fmt

fmt is a simple text formatter that fills and joins lines to make text lines look more uniform in length. It isn't a text processor; it just cleans up files a bit while preserving indents and blank lines.

LINUXspeak

fmt [-w *width*] [*files*]

Option or Argument	Function
-w *width*	Maximum output line length in characters (72 default).
files	Text files to read. If you don't specify any files, stdin is read.

The output of fmt is sent to stdout.

Sample

Suppose that you have been editing a file named my.novel and the lines are all sorts of strange lengths. You can use the following command to make all lines 65 characters long and save a new version in my.new.novel.

fmt -w 65 my.novel >my.new.novel

You can use fmt while you are in vi to reformat text. To reformat the current paragraph, move the cursor to the top of the para-graph, type !fmt}, and press Enter.

Formatting Text with groff

groff is the GNU version of troff, the text formatting system that turned UNIX into something useful for Bell Labs. People have written complete books on troff. I have written this section merely to help you understand what it is and how to print the documents that are formatted in groff on your LINUX system.

✦ groff uses commands embedded in text files to control formatting. They consist of commands that start with a dot (.) plus control sequences that start with a backslash (\).

✦ groff has macro packages that are designed for specific uses: man for manuals, ms and mm for documents, and me for doing your CS thesis at U.C. Berkeley.

✦ groff has preprocessors for handling tables (tbl), equations (eqn), and pictures (pic).

✦ groff has output filters to produce PostScript, dvi, ASCII, and X11 formats.

LINUXspeak

groff [-m*macro*] [-o*pages*] [-t] *files*

Option	Function
-m*macro*	Specifies the macro package: an for man macros, e for me macros, m for mm macros, or s for ms macros.
-o*pages*	You can specify the pages you want to print in a comma delimited list. You specify ranges with a hyphen. Default is all pages.
-t	Preprocesses the document using tbl, a program that allows you to create tables.

The macro packages enhance the groff command set and address a more specific audience than bare groff, as the following table shows:

Macro Package	Use
man	This is the package for producing the documentation included with UNIX and LINUX systems. It is rather basic and very specific to creating a document with the structure of a man page.
me	This package was developed at University of California, Berkeley in the computer science department. It was designed to address the specific needs of producing a thesis. It is, however, much more general than the man package and has been used commercially to produce manuals.
mm	Developed at AT&T, this is the most modern, most general package. It is the best choice for producing books and reports.
ms	Also developed at AT&T, ms is older than mm. It is general purpose but with fewer features than mm. You may want to choose this package because it is less complicated and, therefore, easier to learn than mm.

Sample

All of the LINUX manual pages (man pages) are written using the
man macros. Suppose you decide that you want a hard copy of the
man page for groff, which is named groff.1 because it is in Section
1 of the manual (user commands). You type `locate groff.1`,
press Enter, and find it is in /usr/man/man1. You then enter the
following to print it:

```
cd /usr/man/man1
groff -man groff.1 | lpr
```

Note that on some LINUX systems the man pages are kept in
gzipped format. In that case, the file would be named groff.1.gz and
you would need to use the following command to print it:

```
zcat groff.1.gz | groff -man | lpr
```

groff is just a front-end program for the whole document processing section. For more details, see the man pages on gtroff, gtbl,
geqn, and gpic. For details on the macro packages, check out
groff_me, groff_mm, and groff_ms in Section 7 of the man pages.

Spell-Checking with ispell

ispell is an interactive spelling checker. For me, the best thing
about ispell is that it guesses what you intended to spell.

To spell-check one or more files, enter

`ispell` *filenames*

When ispell finds a word of questionable spelling, it highlights the
word, possibly offers some suggestions, and then waits for you to
tell it what to do. Here are your choices:

Your Input	What It Does
0 - n	Replaces the word with one of the suggested words
Space	Accepts the word this time but, if found in another place in the file, asks again
a	Accepts the word for the rest of this ispell execution
i	Accepts the word and adds it, as is, to your private dictionary
l	Looks up words that match a pattern you specify in the system dictionary
q	Quits ispell without making any updates
r	Replaces the misspelled word with what you enter
u	Accepts the word and adds it, uncapitalized, to your personal dictionary

Your Input	What It Does
x	Makes the updates up to this point, writes out the updated file, and moves on to the next specified file
Ctrl+l	Redraws the screen
!	Escapes to the shell
?	Displays a help message

ispell searches in your home directory and the current directory for your personal dictionary. If it finds a personal dictionary in both places, it merges the two. ispell then names the dictionary .ispell_*something,* in which *something* is the word default (making .ispell_default) or the equivalent for whichever language you are using (such as .ispell_french).

You can build your own *hash tables* for ispell (the lookup tables that enable ispell to find words quickly). If you would like to do this, check out the documentation on buildhash, munchlist, findaffix, tryaffix, icombine, and ijoin on the ispell man page.

ispell includes dictionaries for English, Danish, French, German, Italian, Spanish, Swedish, and perhaps more languages.

While seldom used, ispell has an array of command-line options. My favorites follow:

Option	What It Does
-b	Creates a backup file by appending .bak to the name of the input file
-n	Assumes the input file is in troff format
-p	Uses the file as your personal dictionary
-S	Sorts ispells guesses by probability of correctness instead of alphabetically
-t	Assumes the input file is in TeX or LaTeX format

If you use ispell with TeX or LaTeX, take a look at the man page. ispell treats LaTeX source with surprising intelligence. ispell is familiar enough with LaTeX commands that it doesn't treat them as spelling errors.

## Part VI

Sending and Receiving E-Mail

LINUX grew up on the Internet, so you shouldn't be surprised to find out that it comes with a great assortment of tools for working with e-mail. With Finland's Linus Torvald and thousands of other people worldwide contributing to the LINUX development effort, a wide range of e-mail options were certain to be an essential part of the LINUX system.

In this part . . .

- ✔ Understanding the pieces of an e-mail system
- ✔ Using elm and pine, the most popular screen-based e-mail programs
- ✔ Getting your e-mail remotely with POP
- ✔ Working with metamail files

Collecting All the Pieces

For e-mail to work properly, all its pieces need to fit together. The elm and pine programs offer users an interface for electronic mail, and behind the scenes are programs such as smail and sendmail that handle getting mail messages to the Internet.

For those of you who use a PPP connection to the Internet, there is one more piece you may need — a program that allows you to get your messages using POP. (*PPP* stands for *Point-to-Point Protocol,* a scheme for connecting two computers over a phone line. *POP* stands for *Post Office Protocol,* a system by which a mail server on the Internet lets you pick up your mail and download it to your machine.)

✦ A mail transfer agent (MTA) gets mail from one remote host and transfers the mail to another remote host. Two common MTAs are sendmail and smail.

✦ SMTP, Simple Mail Transfer Protocol, is the language spoken by MTAs.

✦ Post Office Protocol (POP) is an alternative language (alternative to SMTP) spoken by MTAs.

✦ A mail user agent (MUA) sends and receives your mail. Examples of MUAs include elm and pine.

Decoding MIME Messages with munpack

MIME (Multipurpose Internet Mail Extensions) allows almost any type of file to be included within an e-mail message. MIME is an Internet standard described in RFC-1341. (RFC stands for *Request for Comments,* which is a collection of Internet standards papers.) Each attachment to a mail message has its own identifier in a text line that starts with `Content-Type:`. The suggested name for the unencoded file also appears in this line.

Two programs available for LINUX work with MIME encoded messages: metamail and munpack. Metamail is designed to be called by a mail reading program to display the contents of the attachment. munpack is designed to be the command to unpack a MIME message saved into files with the names suggested in the header.

LINUXspeak

`munpack` [`-C` *dir*] [`-f`] [`-q`] [`-t`] [*files*]

Option or Argument	What It Does
`-C dir`	Changes directories to *dir* before reading any files. Useful if you are piping a file into munpack.
`-f`	Overwrites existing files. Without this flag, munpack appends .n where n is an integer.
`-q`	Quiet. Doesn't display uninteresting messages.
`-t`	Writes the text parts of a MIME message to files. By default, text parts that do not have a name specified in the header are discarded.
`files`	MIME format files to unpack. If you don't specify any files, munpack reads the file to unpack from standard input.

metamail uses the file /etc/mailcap to determine how to process the different types of attachments. You may have to tune the entries in /etc/mailcap to reflect your local configuration.

Sample

Suppose that you save a MIME message in a file named strange.stuff. To get an idea what is in the file, you can use `grep` to look for Content-Type: lines:

```
grep "^Content-Type:" strange.stuff
```

If you do so, you get the following output:

```
Content-Type: TEXT/PLAIN; charset-US-ASCII
Content-Type: APPLICATION/octet-stream; name="fig4-
    2.tif"
```

You can then unpack it like so:

```
munpack strange.stuff
```

munpack creates two files: fig4-2.tif and tif4-2.desc. The second file is from the text that munpack associated with the tif file. If you use the -t option, munpack creates a a file named part1 instead.

Dissecting E-Mail Addresses

Just as you need an address to send a letter via snail mail, you need an address in order to send e-mail. A e-mail address is composed of two parts — who and where. An "at" sign (@)separates these two parts. For example, in the mail address phil@ssc.com, phil is the who, and ssc.com is the where.

◆ The portion of the address to the right of the @ is a domain name. It could refer to a set of computers rather than an individual machine.

◆ Levels in the domain name are separated by a dot (`.`).

◆ The top-level domain is the one at the rightmost part of the address. In `phil@ssc.com`, `com` is the top level domain.

◆ Moving to the left in the domain part of the address, each name is a member of the domain to its right. In `phil@ssc.com`, `ssc` is a member of the `com` domain.

◆ Individual computers may have their own names (for example, mine is named `truckin`), but you generally do not need to use the machine name. For example, my official e-mail address is `phil@truckin.ssc.com`, but you can send e-mail to me at `phil@ssc.com`, and I will receive it.

◆ If you are sending e-mail to someone on your machine or local network, you can use just that person's user name (without the `@domain` part of the address).

With all that said, if people give you their complete e-mail addresses in the format just described, and if you are connected to the Internet, you should be able to send them mail.

Managing E-Mail with elm

The elm e-mail program was written by Dave Taylor and is now maintained by a cooperative group. You can start elm when you first log on to your LINUX system and then just keep it running. Simply type `elm` at the shell prompt. elm displays a list of message titles and waits for your instructions.

Strange as it may seem, you get more help if you set your user level to Expert. elm assumes that if you are beginner you want to hear less about what you can do. Use the options menu (`o`) to change the user level.

Creating mail aliases

elm includes a mechanism that allows you to create aliases for mail recipients. So instead of having to remember a mail address such as `Robert.Klazowski@super-duper-systems.com`, you can just use an alias like `bob`.

To create a new alias, follow these steps:

1. From the elm mail index, press **a** to access the aliases menu.

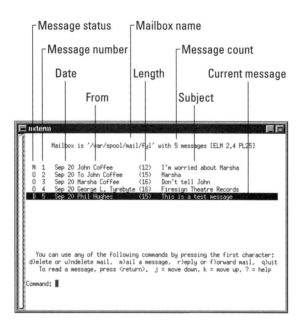

┌─Message status ┌─Mailbox name

┌─Message number ┌─Message count

Date │ Length │ Current message

From │ Subject

2. If you want to create an alias for the person who sent you your current message, press a; otherwise, press n.

3. Type the alias name and, if requested, other information.

4. Press r to exit the alias menu and return to the mail index.

You also can choose these options from the alias menu:

 ✦ d — Delete an alias.

 ✦ m — Mail to an alias. (You don't need to do this from the alias menu. Once an alias exists, you can use it like any other mail address.)

 ✦ / — Search your aliases for the string you enter.

 ✦ e — Edit your alias file using your regular text editor.

Exiting elm

If you want to exit elm and save the changes you made to your mailbox, follow these steps.

1. Press q.

2. Depending on your configuration, elm may ask if you want your messages saved to your received file ($HOME/Mail/received). Generally you want to reply by pressing n so that messages stay in your incoming mailbox.

If you want to exit elm and abandon your changes to your mailbox, follow these steps:

1. Press x.

2. If you have made any changes to your mailbox, elm asks you whether you really want to abandon them.

3. Press y to really give them up or press n if you chicken out.

Getting help

elm has built-in help. To enter the help system, follow these steps:

1. Press ?.

2. If you want help on a particular command, press the command letter. Otherwise, press ? again for general help.

Printing a message

To print an e-mail message, follow these steps:

1. If you are not already in elm, type elm.

2. Use the cursor keys to scroll through the list of messages.

3. Press Enter when the cursor is on the message that you want to print. If the message does not fit on one screen, use Space to move along through the message.

4. Press p.

5. To return to the index, press i.

Your default printer is specified in the options menu. If you want to print on a different printer, use the pipe (|) command within elm. Instead of pressing p, press | and then specify the command you want your file passed through, in this case lpr — the line printer spooler — with options you want. For example, to print an e-mail message on a printer named eggplant, you enter

```
| lpr -P eggplant
```

Reading a message

To read your e-mail messages, follow these steps:

1. If you are not already in elm, type elm.

2. Use the cursor keys to scroll through the list of messages.

3. Press Enter when the cursor is on the message that you want to read. If the message does not fit on one screen, use Space to move along through the message.

4. To return to the index, press i.

Rather than selecting a message with the cursor keys, you can

✦ Search for a keyword in the Subject or From line using / as you do in vi.

✦ Select a particular message by typing its number and then pressing Enter.

✦ Search the body of the messages for a string by typing / / and typing the string, and then pressing Enter.

Reading other mail files

By default, elm accesses your incoming mail file. This file is known as /var/spool/mail/*name,* where *name* corresponds to your login name. To make elm read from another file, follow these steps:

1. Press c. elm prompts you with Change to which folder:.

2. Enter the name of the file you want to read and press Enter. You can type =name to specify a file named *name* in your $HOME/Mail directory.

If you want elm to read a different mail file when you start it, you can specify a filename using the -f option. For example, to read mail from the file ~garbonzo/Mail/beans, enter elm -f ~garbonzo/ Mail/beans.

Saving a message

By default, elm saves e-mail in the $HOME/Mail directory. elm assumes you usually want to save messages in the directory whose name matches the name of the sender. You specify the directory in which you want elm to save your messages by preceding the filename with an =.

Follow these steps to save an e-mail message:

1. If you are not already in elm, type elm.

2. Use the cursor keys or a search to find the message you want to save.

3. Press s.

4. elm suggests a filename. If you like the suggestion, just press Enter. Otherwise, type the filename you want and press Enter. If the file already exists, elm appends the message to the file.

elm saves messages in mailbox format. That means that if you save multiple messages to a file, you can read them individually using elm.

Sending a message

If you want to send an e-mail message with elm, follow these steps:

1. If you are not already in elm, type e l m.

2. Press m. (Elm automatically starts the editor for you.) elm then asks you to fill in the addressee information.

3. Enter any number of mail addresses, each separated by a space, in the To: line and press Enter. elm asks you for a subject.

4. Enter a subject in the Subject: line.

5. If elm asks you whether you want anyone to receive a copy of the message, enter additional addresses in the Cc: line. Just press Enter if you don't want anyone else to receive a copy.

6. Type your message, save it (how you do save this message depends on which editor you have — type ZZ if you use vi). The file is saved to a temporary file; you can save it to a permanent file by using the command shown in the following table.

7. Exit the editor.

8. Choose from among the following options for what to do next with the message:

Command	What It Does
c	Saves a copy of the message in a specified file.
e	Reenters the text editor to continue editing the message.
f	Forgets it — throws away the message.
h	Edits the message headers. You can, for example, choose to have someone receive a blind carbon copy of your message.
i	Spell checks the message with ispell.
p	PGP (Pretty Good Privacy) encrypts the message.
s	Sends the message on its way.
!	Escapes to a shell.

Tagging messages

You may at times want to save or print a whole set of messages to one place. Rather than individually saving each message, you can tag them. The save command then works with the tagged messages instead of just the current message. To tag a message, follow these steps:

1. Move to the message by using the arrow keys or by entering the message number.

2. Press t. A + sign appears to the left of the message number to indicate that it is tagged.

To untag an already tagged message, press t again.

Using elm options

elm is very configurable. To change its basic options, you must use the options menu. To edit an option, follow these steps:

1. Enter the letter shown at the left of the option you want to change.

2. If the option is a selection from a set of values press Space until the desired value appears and then press Enter. Otherwise, type the new value and press Enter.

3. Press > to make your option changes permanent, or press i to discard your changes.

Managing E-Mail with pine

pine evolved from elm. It was designed to be idiot-proofed and comes pretty close. (pine, by the way, is copyrighted by the University of Washington.) But pine tends to frustrate more serious users because by default it assumes that you don't know what you are doing and that you need to ask a lot of questions.

pine outdoes elm in one important way: In pine you can seamlessly attach other types of files to your mail message. (These attachments are known as *metamail attachments.*)

When you invoke pine, it changes directories to your home directory. Therefore, if you need to enter a file name (for an attachment, for example), you must enter its pathname relative to your home directory rather than the directory that was current when you invoked pine. If you need help locating a file press Ctrl+T to start pine's file navigator.

Exiting pine

When you want to exit pine, simply follow these steps:

1. Press q. pine asks you whether you really want to quit.

2. If you are sure that you want to quit, press y.

Printing a message

To print an e-mail message, follow these steps:

1. If you are not already in pine, type `pine`.

2. Press 1 to go to your folder list.

3. Use the arrow keys to highlight the desired folder and press Enter.

4. Use the arrow keys to highlight the desired message.

5. Press y.

The default printer is defined in the pine configuration menu. Press s from the main menu to access the printer configuration menu.

Reading a message

Follow these steps to read your e-mail messages in pine:

1. If you are not already in pine, type `pine`.

2. Press 1 to go to your folder list.

3. Use the arrow keys to highlight the desired folder (`INBOX` to read your incoming mail) and press Enter.

4. Use the arrow keys to highlight the desired message.

5. Press Enter to view the message.

Saving a message

By default, pine saves messages in the $HOME/mail directory. To save a message, follow these steps:

1. If you are not already in pine, type `pine`.

2. Press 1 to go to your folder list.

3. Use the arrow keys to highlight the desired folder and press Enter.

4. Use the arrow keys to highlight the desired message.

5. Press s.

6. Type the desired filename and press Enter.

Sending a message

To send a message with pine, follow these steps:

1. If you are not already in pine, type `pine`.

2. Press c (for compose). pine asks you for the addressees.

3. Enter any number of mail addresses, each separated by a comma, next to To: and press Enter. pine asks whether you want to send a copy of the message to anyone.

4. Enter any additional mail addresses of people who should receive copies, each separated by a comma, and press Enter. If you do not want anyone to receive a copy, just press Enter.

5. If you want to attach a file, enter the file's name (as described in the following section) next to Attchmnt:, or just press Enter.

6. Enter a subject next to Subject:, or just press Enter. You can then enter your message.

7. When you are finished composing your message, press Ctrl+X to send the message.

You can press Ctrl+G at any time to receive context-sensitive help.

Working with attachments

An *attachment* is a nontext file such as a graphic that you mail without having to manipulate it into something that the mail system thinks is text. In pine, you only need to identify the file you want to attach, and pine takes care of packaging it.

To attach a file, enter the name of the file when you receive the Attchmnt: prompt, or follow these steps to attach a file at any time:

1. Press Ctrl+J. pine prompts you with File to attach: and a mini-menu.

2. If you know the file name, enter it. Otherwise, press Ctrl+T to start the file navigator and select the file you want to attach. pine prompts you with Attachment comment:.

3. Enter any comment you might want to include in the file and press Enter. If you don't have a comment, just press Enter.

If you want to add another attachment, just press Ctrl+J again and follow the rest of the steps.

If you intend to use both elm and pine, you should link the Mail and mail directories. elm uses Mail, and pine uses mail. If you link them, all your saved mail appears in the same directory.

Using fetchmail for Remote Mail Access

If you don't have a dedicated connection to the Internet and want a way to download your incoming e-mail, you should try Post Office Protocol (POP). You can run a client program on your local system and tell it to fetch your mail.

The most popular of the client programs is called fetchmail; another is called popclient.

TIP

You can automate downloading your mail by adding a call to fetchmail to your PPP connect script.

LINUXspeak

```
fetchmail [-c] [-d secs] [-f mfile] [-k] [-m] [-p
    proto] [-u username]
```

Option or Argument	What It Does
-c	Checks for mail and reports. Doesn't fetch any messages.
-d	Runs as a daemon and fetches mail every *secs* seconds. If you have started fetchmail in this mode and want to terminate it, type fetchmail --quit to kill the daemon.
-f rcfile	Specifies the location of the fetchmail run control file ($HOME/.fetchmailrc default).
-k	Keeps retrieved message on the remote server. Handy for testing.
-m	Passes mail to the MDA directly (instead of forwarding it via port 25).
-p proto	The protocol to use when retrieving mail. **See** the following table for your choices.
-u username	The login name to use on the mail server. This defaults to your login name on your local machine.

The following table lists your mail retrieval protocol choices.

Protocol	Meaning
IMAP	IMAP2bis
POP2	Post Office Protocol 2
POP3	Post Office Protocol 3
APOP	POP3 with MD5 authentication
KPOP	POP3 with Kerberos authentication

POP3 is the most common POP protocol. Check with your internal service provider for the best choice.

WEIRDNESS

If you elect to use the -m option, make sure you don't use an option that forces your MDA to interpret the To, Cc, and Bcc lines (such as -t in sendmail). This option causes a mail loop.

## Part VII

Working with the Other Guys

Although some of us LINUX fanatics think it should be the only operating system out there, we have to live with the fact that it's not — yet. In order to blend in with the rest of the computer world, you must be able to deal with at least MS-DOS files and media, and preferably other non-LINUX media. That's what this part is all about.

In this part . . .

- ✔ Working with MS-DOS files and media
- ✔ Working with Macintosh media
- ✔ Working with UNIX files and media
- ✔ Converting data using LINUX utilities

Working with MS-DOS Media

You can work with MS-DOS files in either one of two ways: by using what are called Mtools, or by mounting the disk and just using regular LINUX commands.

Mtools Basics

Mtools are a series of commands specifically written to act like the standard MS-DOS file manipulation commands. They are called Mtools because they designed to work with MS-DOS files. The actual command names are just the MS-DOS command names with an m in front of them.

✦ Mtools support VFAT (long style) filenames. If the specified filename does not fit into the standard 8.3 format of MS-DOS, Mtools create a VFAT name and an appropriate short name. The original name is called the *primary name;* any derived name is called the *secondary name.*

✦ You refer to the MS-DOS filesystems by device names. By default, A is the first floppy disk, B is the second, J is a Jaz drive (if available), and Z is a Zip drive (if available).

✦ Mtools wildcards work the way they work in LINUX. That is, the * character matches all files as it would with LINUX, unlike MS-DOS in which you have to use * . *.

✦ Precede filenames with a drive letter and a colon (for example, you can use **a:**) to tell Mtools that the files are on an MS-DOS device. Otherwise Mtools assumes they are on the LINUX filesystem.

✦ Mtools supports most high-capacity disk format schemes.

✦ You use the /usr/local/etc/mtools.conf and $HOME/.mtoolsrc configuration files to configure Mtools.

All the Mtools programs use the following command line options. Check out the mtools.1 man page for complete configuration information.

Option	Function
-a	Renames the primary name if there is a conflict
-A	Renames the secondary name if there is a conflict
-m	Asks the user what to do with the primary name on conflict
-M	Asks the user what to do with the secondary name on conflict
-o	Overwrites the primary name if there is a conflict

Option	Function
-O	Overwrites the secondary name if there is a conflict
-s	Skips the primary name if there is a conflict
-S	Skips the secondary name if there is a conflict

mcd — Changing the current directory

You use mcd to change the current directory on the MS-DOS device. The current information is saved in $HOME/.mcwd.

LINUXspeak

mcd [*dos_dir*]

Argument	Function
dos_dir	Name of an MS-DOS directory and/or device to make current. If you do not specify a directory or device, mcd returns the name of the current directory.

mcopy — Copying files between DOS disks

The mcopy command copies files to and from DOS disks. It also handles any necessary filename conversions in the process (because of the limitations on filename length in MS-DOS).

LINUXspeak

mcopy [-m] [-n] [-Q] [-t] *source target*
mcopy [-m] [-n] [-t] *dos_source*

Option or Argument	Function
-m	Preserves file modification time.
-n	Overwrites files without asking for confirmation.
-Q	Quits if any file copy fails.
-t	Text transfer. Converts Return/Newline sequence to Newline only.
source	A file or files to copy from. If you specify multiple files, *target* must be a directory.
target	Destination file for single file copies or a destination directory if you specify multiple files.
dos_source	A file on an MS-DOS disk. mcopy copies the file to a file of the same name in the current LINUX directory.

mdel — Deleting MS-DOS files

The equivalent to the del command on MS-DOS, mdel deletes one or more files from an MS-DOS disk.

LINUXspeak

mdel [-v] *dos_files*

Option or Argument	Function
-v	Verbose mode
dos_files	Names of files to delete

mdir — Displaying an MS-DOS directory

mdir is the equivalent of the MS-DOS command dir. The -w option is equivalent to the /w switch of the dir command.

LINUXspeak

mdir [-w] *dos_dir*
mdir [-a] [-f] [-w] *dos_files*

Option or Argument	Function
-a	Includes hidden files in the list
-f	Fast output — doesn't include freespace count
-w	Wide output — lists filenames with no size or date information
dos_dir	Name of the directory whose contents are to be listed
dos_file	MS-DOS filenames (possibly using wildcard notation)

minfo — Printing MS-DOS file system parameters

minfo displays the content of the fields of the boot sector of an MS-DOS file system.

LINUXspeak

minfo [-v] *drive*

Option or Argument	Function
-v	Includes a hex dump of the boot sector.
drive	Drive designator (a:, b:, ...) of the device to access.

mmd — *Making a new directory*

The mmd command makes one or more directories on the MS-DOS disk.

LINUXspeak

mmd *dos_dirs*

Argument	Fuction
dos_dirs	Directory names or drive letters followed by : and directory names to create.

mtype — *Displaying file contents*

The command mtype displays the contents of a file on the screen. It also has options to do some minor translations during the display process.

LINUXspeak

mtype [-s] [-t] *dos_files*

Option or Argument	Function
-s	Strips the high bit from the data
-t	Translates Return/Newline to Newline
dos_files	Names of files to display

mcopy does not allow you to append files as its MS-DOS equivalent does. To append files, use mtype and redirect its output to a file. For example, to append two.nd onto the end of fir.st from the first floppy and put the result in both.files, type mtype a:fir.st a:two.nd > both.files.

xcopy — *Copying one directory to another*

xcopy reproduces the file hierarchy under one directory in another location by copying all the files and subdirectories.

LINUXspeak

xcopy *source_dir target_dir*

Argument	Function
source_dir	Directory of files to copy.
target_dir	Destination of copy. If *target_dir* does not exist, xcopy creates it and the files are copied directly into it.

More Mtools commands

The following commands are also included in the Mtools utilities.

Command	Function
mattrib	Sets/clears attribute bits
mbadblocks	Scans for bad blocks
mdeltree	Deletes a directory tree
mformat	Formats an MS-DOS disk
minfo	Displays the content of the fields of the boot sector of an MS-DOS file system
mkmanifest	Creates a LINUX shell script to unmangle the MS-DOS conversion to 8.3 filenames
mlabel	Adds a volume label
mmount	Mounts MS-DOS file system
mmove	Renames an MS-DOS file or directory
mpartition	Creates an MS-DOS partition
mrd	Removes an MS-DOS subdirectory
mren	Renames an MS-DOS file or directory
mtoolstest	Tests Mtools configuration

Mounting MS-DOS Media and Partitions

Rather than using Mtools, you can use the support for MS-DOS file systems that is built into LINUX. You mount the MS-DOS file system just like any other file system, and then you treat it like part of the LINUX file hierarchy.

Mounting hard disk partitions

If you have an MS-DOS file system on your LINUX computer, you can keep it mounted. Just follow these steps:

1. Log on as root.

2. Create a mount point directory using mkdir.

3. Edit /etc/fstab and add a mount line for the appropriate device and mount point. See the following table for examples of the fields in this line.

4. Save the updated version of /etc/fstab.

5. Type mount -a to force a reread of /etc/fstab.

Field	Function
Device	The device name of the partition.
Mount point	Name of the directory where the file system is to be mounted.
Filesystem type	Type of file system to mount. Use msdos for an MS-DOS partition.
Options	How it should be mounted. Using default is safe.
Dump frequency	Use 0 if you don't want this partition to be included in standard dumps.
Fsck order	Use 0.

For example, if your second partition on your first hard drive (/dev/hda2) has an MS-DOS file system on it and you want it to be automatically mounted in the directory /dosC whenever you boot up LINUX, add this line to /etc/fstab.

```
/dev/hda2   /dosC msdos  default      0      0
```

You can back up MS-DOS filesystems by mounting them under LINUX and then using LINUX backup utilities such as tar or cpio to back them up.

Mounting and unmounting removable media

The following command mounts an MS-DOS floppy in a directory called /mnt/dos. Make sure the directory /mnt/dos exists before attempting the mount.

```
mount -t msdos /mnt/dos /dev/fd0
```

To unmount it, make sure you are no longer in any directory on the disk. The command is:

```
umount /mnt/dos
```

If you add an entry to /etc/fstab for your floppy device and allow user mount, then any user can mount and umount MS-DOS disks. For example, the command should look like

```
/dosA /dev/fd0 msdos user,noauto 0 0
```

Users can then mount a floppy by typing mount /dosA.

Working with Mac Media

You can use a set of tools similar to Mtools to work with Mac HFS volumes (the standard Macintosh file system). You must first mount the HFS volume using hmount; then you can use all the other utilities to work with the data.

hcd — *Changing the hfs working directory*

hcd changes the current working directory on the Mac disk.

LINUXspeak

hcd [hfs_path]

Argument	Function
hfs_path	Directory on HFS volume you want to make the current working directory. If you do not specify the path, hcd changes the current directory to the root of the volume.

hcopy — *Copying files to or from an hfs volume*

hcopy copies files between Mac disks and LINUX file systems. You can instruct hcopy how to treat the two parts of the Mac file when it performs the copy.

LINUXspeak

hcopy [-a|-b|-m|-r|-t] sources target

Option or Argument	Function
-a	Automatic — mcopy guesses the right translation (default).
-b	BinHex — an alternative format to -m for binary data.
-m	MacBinary II — copies both forks of the Mac file. Good choice for arbitrary Mac files.
-r	Raw data — copies only the data fork with no translation.
-t	Text — copies only the data fork of the Mac file and performs end-of-line translation.
sources	Files to copy. You specify stdin by using a -. Use a : at the beginning to force an HFS path; use . / at the beginning to force a LINUX path.
target	Destination file or directory. Specify stdout by using a -. Use a : at the beginning to force an HFS path; use a . / at the beginning to force a LINUX path.

hdel — *Deleting files from an HFS volume*

Use the hdel command to delete one or more files from the current Macintosh volume.

LINUXspeak

hdel hfs_paths

Argument	Function
hfs_paths	The name of the file or files to delete, relative to the current directory on the HFS volume

hdir — Listing the files in an HFS directory

hdir displays a listing of the files in the current directory or a specified directory.

LINUXspeak
hdir [*hfs_path*]

Argument	Function
hfs_path	Pathname of the directory to list. The current working directory is used if you do not specify the hfs_path.

hmkdir — Creating a new directory

Use the command hmkdir to create new directories on the current Mac disk.

LINUXspeak
hmkdir *hfs_paths*

Argument	Function
hfs_paths	Pathname of the directories to create

hmount — Mounting an HFS volume

You must use hmount to mount a Mac HFS volume before you can use any of the other commands that access the volume.

LINUXspeak
hmount *source_path* [*part*]

Argument	Function
source_path	LINUX pathname to a block device or regular file containing an HFS volume image.
part	Use partition number part as the partition to mount. If you not specify, the first HFS partition is mounted.

humount — Unmounting an HFS volume

You generally do not need to use the humount command. It only updates $HOME/.hcwd.

LINUXspeak

hunmount [*volume*]

Argument	Function
volume	The volume name or path to the HFS volume to unmount. If you do not specify, the current HFS volume is unmounted.

Other hfsutils commands

The following HFS utility programs are also available.

Command	Function
hattrib	Changes file or directory attributes
hformat	Creates a new HFS filesystem
hfs	Shell for manipulating HFS volumes
hls	Lists the files in an HFS directory
hpwd	Prints working directory name of current HFS volume
hrename	Renames an HFS file or directory
hrmdir	Removes an empty HFS directory
hvol	Displays or change the current HFS volume
xhfs	Graphical interface to HFS commands

Working with UNIX Files and Media

You should have no problem working with UNIX file and media. The POSIX standard that LINUX complies with is based on UNIX. With careful use of options on utilities such as tar and cpio, you should be able to transfer files between UNIX and LINUX systems without a hitch.

## Part VIII

Networking

The Internet, the largest and most well-known networking system, is really what made LINUX happen. Without the Internet, the cooperative effort that went into developing LINUX wouldn't have been possible. So, it only stands to reason that LINUX provides you with the means to exchange data with the wide world of computer users.

In this part . . .

- ✔ Transferring files over a network
- ✔ Working interactively on remote machines
- ✔ Checking network connectivity

Deciphering Network Addressing

Computers on any network (the Internet being the biggest example) use an assortment of network addressing methods. For a more detailed look at network addressing, check out *Linux SECRETS* (IDG Books Worldwide, Inc.) or the *Linux Network Administrators Manual* available on the LINUX Documentation pages (click <u>LDP</u> on www.linuxresources.com).

Domain addresses

Rather than having to remember the IP address of a computer system, we humans would rather remember a name. That's when domains come in handy. A *domain* is a symbolic name that can be used to refer to a particular IP address.

Multiple domain names can refer to the same IP address, and multiple domain names can refer to different IP addresses on the same machine. Check out www.linuxjournal.com and www.linuxresources.com as an example. These two URLs take you to the same machine but on a different home page.

To establish a domain name you need to register with the Internic at rs.internic.net.

IP addresses

All machines on the Internet (and most likely on your local network as well) have IP (Internet Protocol) addresses. An IP address is composed of four numbers, each ranging from zero to 255 that are written in *dotted quad notation.* This means that the four numbers are written as a string with dots separating each of them. For example, 198.186.207.128 is the IP address of one of my computers.

Companies are assigned IP addresses in blocks. For example, all the addresses in the block 198.186.207 (with the last value being 0 through 255) are mine. This is called a Class C address.

It is possible, and sometimes desirable, to have multiple IP addresses assigned to the same machine. A common use for this is when you want your Web server to do something differently depending on the address you access it from (display a different home page, for example).

Nameservers

When you register your domain name you need to specify the IP addresses of at least two *nameservers* (machines that have the information necessary to map your domain name to the IP address of the computer that the message should be delivered to). Nameservers must be able to respond to queries from other nameservers so that the name-to-address translation is available wherever needed. Mapping between IP addresses and hardware addresses is handled by Address Resolution Protocol (ARP) and Reverse ARP.

ftp — *Transferring Files*

FTP (*file transfer protocol)* is the most common way to send and receive files over the Internet. You can also use it on a local network. (Just to avoid some ftp-versus-FTP confusion, *ftp* is the name of the program in LINUX and *FTP* is the general process.)

To use FTP, you need an account on a remote machine. You can log in to many public servers with the user name *anonymous* and send and receive files.

LINUXspeak

`ftp` [-d] [-g] [-i] [-n] [-v] [*host*]

Option or Argument	Function
-d	Enables debug mode.
-g	Disables wildcard expansion of file names (also known as *globbing* in UNIXspeak).
-i	Turns off interactive prompting during multifile transfers.
-n	Instructs program not to attempt auto-login. ftp normally prompts you with a guess at your login name and allows you to press Enter if you are happy with it. In this mode no login attempt is made and you will have to type **user** at the ftp> prompt to log in.
-v	Shows all responses from the remote server and transfer statistics.
host	The name of the machine you want to connect to. If you omit host, ftp asks you for the machine name.

Connecting to anonymous FTP servers

An anonymous FTP session is just like a regular FTP session except you don't need your own account. Many servers (such as sunsite.unc.edu) offer anonymous FTP so you can access publicly available files. For example, all of LINUX is available via anonymous FTP from Sunsite and hundreds of other anonymous FTP servers.

Follow these steps to connect to an anonymous FTP server:

1. At your shell prompt, type **ftp** followed by the name of the remote system.

2. When prompted for a login name, type **anonymous**.

3. When prompted for a password, enter your e-mail address. You then get a message that you're logged in.

Most systems offer a program named ncftp. It offers a friendlier interface that includes a bookmark file where you can save your favorite FTP sites and logins. To see if ncftp is available, type **ncftp** at your shell prompt. If it comes up, type **help** to display the help screen.

Connecting to the remote system

You can connect to the remote system by following these steps:

1. At the shell prompt, type **ftp** followed by the name of the remote system. ftp then asks you for your user name and password.

2. Type your name and password, and you should receive a message indicating that you are logged in.

A sample login session looks like this:

```
[fyl@smiley fyl]$ ftp orange.fylz.com
Connected to orange.fylz.com.
220 orange.fylz.com FTP server ready.
Name (orange:fyl): fyl
331 Password required for fyl.
Password: enter_password_here
230 User fyl logged in.
Remote system type is UNIX.
Using binary mode to transfer files.
ftp>
```

Configuring .netrc for automatic logins

When you start up the ftp program, it looks for a file named .netrc in your home directory. ftp uses the information .netrc contains to automatically log in to remote machines.

You can create .netrc with your text editor. Each line consists of the following:

```
machine mname login lname password passwd
```

String	Meaning
mname	The machine name of the remote system (for example, `ftp.ssc.com`)
lname	Your login name for this machine
passwd	Your password for this machine

You can place a line at the end of .netrc to instruct ftp to try a login as `anonymous` if the name of the remote system is not in the file.

```
default login anonymous password me@myhost.com
```

Make sure you set the permissions so that only you can read and write to your .netrc file (*see* Part III for more information). Anyone who accesses this file has your passwords for all the machines you use. If you have doubts about system security, don't use .netrc.

Downloading files with ftp

When you download, retrieve, or get files, you transfer them from the remote machine to your local machine. Follow these steps to download files:

1. Use the `cd` command and `dir` command to locate the files you want to download.

2. Set your file transfer mode to match the type of files you intend to retrieve. To do this, type `asc` to set the mode to ASCII for text files or type `bin` for non-ASCII files.

3. Type **get**, then type the name of the file you want to retrieve, and optionally, a new name for the file on the local system. If you omit the new name, the local file will have the same name as the remote file.

For example, this session retrieves the NOTES file from the current directory on the remote system and saves it in /tmp/new.notes on your local system:

```
ftp> get NOTES /tmp/new.notes
local: /tmp/new.notes remote: NOTES
200 PORT command successful.
150 Opening BINARY mode data connection for NOTES
    (4157 bytes).
226 Transfer complete.
4157 bytes received in 0.0269 secs (1.5e+02 Kbytes/
    sec)
```

In ASCII mode, ftp performs line-end conversions (such as translating MS-DOS's Return/Newline sequence to NewlineLINUX). If local and remote systems use the same operating system

(LINUX or UNIX on both ends), you can safely use bin mode for all file transfers.

Executing local commands while in ftp

Sometimes you need to check something on your local machine (such as what directory you are in) while you are in ftp. To do this, just type ! followed by the shell command you want to execute locally.

You may be tempted to use the ! command to change directories on the local machine. However, you can't do it because ! creates a subshell. Once the command is executed, the subshell terminates and you are right back where you started. Use the lcd command to change your local directory.

Exiting ftp

To disconnect from the remote system and exit the ftp program, type **quit**.

ftp command summary

ftp offers a whole assortment of commands. Here is a quick summary of the more interesting ones.

Command	Meaning
asc	Sets ASCII transfer mode.
bin	Sets binary transfer mode.
case	Converts the case of filenames from upper- to lowercase or from lower- to uppercase.
cd *dir*	Changes directories on the remote machine.
delete *file*	Deletes file on the remote system.
dir [*files*] [*dest*]	Lists the names of files matching the pattern *files* (all files default) on the remote system. The output is placed in *dest* on the local system if specified, otherwise it appears on the screen.
get *rfile* [*lfile*]	Transfers *rfile* on the remote system to *lfile* on the local system. *lfile* defaults to the same name as *rfile*.
hash	Turns on/off a pound sign (#) printing on the screen every 1,024 characters.
lcd *dir*	Changes directories on the local system.
mget *files*	Gets the specified files from the remote system.
mput *files*	Puts the specified files onto the remote system.

Command	Meaning
prompt	Toggles prompting mode for the mget and mput commands.
pwd	Displays the name of the current directory on the remote system.
quit	Exits ftp.
verbose	Toggles ftp's verbose message mode.
?	Prints help message. Follow with the name of a command for a help message on that specific command.

Listing directory contents with ftp

Once you are connected to a remote system with ftp, you need to look for what you want. Type dir, and ftp presents you with a listing of the files in the current directory.

You can use two optional arguments to make the listing more specific:

Argument	Meaning
files	A pattern for file selection. Use * if you want to list every file. Use dir ve*, for example, if you want a list of all filenames that begin with ve. This pattern matching works like shell wildcards. (**See** Part II for more details.)
destination	This is the name of a file on your local system. If you use this argument, dir sends its output to the file on your computer instead of displaying it on the screen.

If the directory contains more files than will fit on the screen, you can view the list one page at a time by typing dir * |more. Press Space when you want to see the next page.

Navigating the remote host with ftp

Once you know what is on the remote host, you may need to change directories on that machine. The command is called cd and it works just like the cd shell command on LINUX. You can use relative or absolute pathnames to specify your destination directory. For example, to move to the /pub/Linux/Goodies directory, type cd /pub/Linux/Goodies.

On most anonymous FTP servers, all the action starts at the /pub directory (which is almost always where all the publicly accessible files are located).

Transferring multiple files with ftp

Quite often you want to transfer all the files in a directory or all the files matching a particular pattern:

✦ To upload all the files in your current directory, type `mput *`.

✦ To download all the files in the current directory on the remote system, type `mget *`.

✦ You can type a list of filenames, rather than just the `*` character, if you want to be selective.

✦ `mget` and `mput` ask about each file before they transfer it. Press `y` to transfer the file or `n` to skip it.

✦ If you know you want to transfer everything that matches, type `prompt` to turn off prompting.

Uploading files with ftp

Uploading or sending files to the remote computer is just like downloading except the files are going the other way. Follow these steps to upload files:

1. Use the `cd` command to move to the directory where you want to upload the files.

2. If you are not in the directory on the local machine where the files are located, type `lcd` followed by a directory name to change directories.

3. Set your file transfer mode to match the type of files you intend to retrieve. To do this, type `asc` to set the mode to ASCII for text files or type `bin` for non-ASCII files.

4. Type `put`, the name of the file you want to upload, and optionally, a new name for the file on the remote system. If you omit the new name, the remote file will have the same name as the local file.

Uploading and downloading can take a lot of time over a PPP connection. If you want a status report as progress is made, type `hash` at the `ftp>` prompt. You then see a `#` after each group of 1,024 characters is transferred. Type `hash` again to turn off this command.

nslookup — Querying Internet Name Servers

The nslookup program displays the current information available at a nameserver.

LINUXspeak

```
nslookup [-option] [host]
nslookup [-option] host server
nslookup [-option] - server
```

Option or Argument	Function
-option	Any of the set options (see the following table). You can enter multiple options. You must place a prefix before each option and enter each in the form *keyword=value*.
host	Hostname to look up. If you don't specify *host*, nslookup enters interactive mode.
server	Nameserver to use for the lookup.

If you attempt a lookup using nslookup host and you get a > prompt, your version of nslookup does not support this mode. Abort nslookup (use your kill character or press Ctrl+D). Then type nslookup and press Enter.

nslookup supports the following options. You enter them on the command line or following the keyword set while in interactive mode.

Option	Meaning
all	Displays the current values of common options to set.
domain=*name*	Changes the default domain to *name*. This is the name appended to queries that do not specify a domain.
querytype=*type*	Changes the type of records searched. The default is A (for address records). Other commons values are CNAME (for canonical name for an alias), MX (for mail exchanger), and ANY (to indicate a search of all record types).

Once in interactive mode, you can use the following commands:

Command	Function
exit	Returns to the shell.
finger	Connects to the host that was most recently looked up successfully using the finger server. You can redirect the output of this command using the standard shell > and >> redirection operators.
help	Displays a command summary.
ls *domain*	Lists the information available for *domain*. You can redirect the output of this command using the standard shell > and >> redirection operators.

(continued)

(continued)

Command	Function
lserver *domain*	Changes name servers to *domain*. This command uses the initial server to perform the lookup.
server *domain*	Changes name servers to *domain*. This command uses the current server to perform the lookup.

Sample

In the following example, I first type nslookup with no options, then press Enter to enter interactive mode with the default nameserver. I then type pacificbeachwa.com to look up any records for pacificbeach.com registered with the nameserver. I then do the query with the default search (address record), set the query type to any record by typing querytype=ANY, and repeat the lookup.

```
Default Server: hendrix.aa.net
Address: 204.157.220.4
> pacificbeachwa.com
Server: hendrix.aa.net
Address: 204.157.220.4
Name: pacificbeachwa.com
Address: 199.184.169.73
> set querytype=ANY
> pacificbeachwa.com
Server: hendrix.aa.net
Address: 204.157.220.4
Non-authoritative answer:
pacificbeachwa.com nameserver = UNCLE.SSC.COM
pacificbeachwa.com nameserver = BROKEDOWN.SSC.COM
pacificbeachwa.com internet address =
    199.184.169.73
Authoritative answers can be found from:
pacificbeachwa.com nameserver = UNCLE.SSC.COM
pacificbeachwa.com nameserver = BROKEDOWN.SSC.COM
UNCLE.SSC.COM internet address = 204.157.223.65
BROKEDOWN.SSC.COM internet address = 204.157.223.78
>exit
```

ping — Sending Test Packets to Network Hosts

You can use ping to check the connectivity to another machine. It sends a continuous stream of ICMP (Internet Control Message Protocol) packets to the host you specify and then displays what happened. You see a summary when ping completes the job — either because it has sent the number of packets you requested or because you interrupted the job.

LINUXspeak

```
ping [-c count] [-i secs] [-q] host
```

Option or Argument	Function
-c count	Stops after sending count packets. If you use the default, ping continues until you interrupt it.
-i secs	Waits secs seconds between sending each packet. Default is one second.
-q	Quiet. Only display a summary when ping completes.
host	Name or IP address of the machine you want to send the packets to.

Sample

The following example tells ping to send four packets to
beach1.fylz.com and shows the result of the request.

```
ping -c 4 beach1.fylz.com
PING beach1.fylz.com (198.186.207.200): 56 data
    bytes
64 bytes from 198.186.207.200: icmp_seq=0 ttl=64
    time=1.1 ms
64 bytes from 198.186.207.200: icmp_seq=1 ttl=64
    time=1.0 ms
64 bytes from 198.186.207.200: icmp_seq=2 ttl=64
    time=1.0 ms
64 bytes from 198.186.207.200: icmp_seq=3 ttl=64
    time=0.9 ms

— beach1.fylz.com ping statistics —
4 packets transmitted, 4 packets received, 0%
    packet loss
round-trip min/avg/max = 0.9/1.0/1.1 ms
```

rcp — Copying Remote Files

You can use rcp to copy files between UNIX and LINUX systems on
a local network. To work without the need for passwords, the two
machines must be in each other's host equivalent files.

LINUXspeak

```
rcp [-p] oldfile newfile
rcp [-p] -r oldfiles newdirectory
```

Option or Argument	Meaning
-p	Preserves file modification times
-r	Recursive — copies files in subdirectories
oldfile	Source file to copy
newfile	Destination of copy
newdirectory	Directory where files are to be placed

You can include machine and user names in the descriptions of oldfile, newfile, and newdirectory.

Format	Meaning
host:file	file in your home directory on host
host:~path	file at a specified location relative to your home directory on host
host:~ruser/path	file at specified location relative to home directory of ruser on host
host:/path	file at specified location relative to the root directory on host
ruser@host:path	file at location path relative to the home directory of ruser on host

Sample

To copy the papaya file from your current directory on the local machine to the favorite file in the FruitBasket directory, which is a subdirectory of your home directory on a machine named fruit.fylz.com, use this:

```
rcp papaya fruit.fylz.com:~FruitBasket/favorite
```

rlogin — Logging in Remotely

You can use rlogin to start a terminal session on a remote computer. You can also use telnet (see "telnet — Logging in Remotely" later in this part). If the remote host supports rlogin, use it.

LINUXspeak

```
rlogin [-8] [-E] [- e echar] [-l uname] host
```

Option or Argument	Function
-8	Enables an 8-bit clean data path except for the escape character. The default strips the high bit of each character.
-E	Disables the escape character. When you use it with the -8 option, you get an 8-bit clean data path.
-l *uname*	Sets the login name on the remote system to *uname*. The default is your current login name on the local system.
host	Name of the remote computer.

You can create a link from rlogin to a machine name. If you create the link, you can just type the name of the machine (rather than having to type rlogin followed by the machine you want to connect to) at the shell prompt. For example, if the rlogin program is /usr/bin/rlogin you could, as systems administrator, create a link to it from /usr/local/bin/tofu with the command ln -s /usr/bin/login /usr/local/bin/tofu. Ordinary users could then type **tofu** to invoke rlogin and tell it they wanted to log in to a machine known as tofu.

Connecting to the remote host using rlogin

You can use the rlogin program to connect to the remote host by following these steps:

1. Type **rlogin** and the name of the remote computer.

2. Enter your password if your machine is not in /etc/hosts.equiv on the remote system.

You are now running a shell on the remote machine and can enter shell commands as you would on your local machine.

Terminating your rlogin session

Your rlogin session is just like any other shell session. Type **exit** or **logout** to end the session.

rsh — Executing Commands Remotely

You can use rsh it to do about the same things that you use rlogin to do, but you also can use rsh to execute a single command on a remote system.

If you remotely log in to a system over the Internet, look into obtaining a copy of ssh. It works much like rsh but encrypts the data.

LINUXspeak

`rsh [-l user] [-n] [host] [command]`

Option or Argument	Function
`-l user`	Sets login name on the remote system to *user*. The default is your current login name on the local system.
`-n`	Redirects standard input from `/dev/null`. This means that if the program you are executing remotely attempts to read from standard input, it will receive an end of file.
`command`	The shell command to run on the remote computer. If you don't specify a *command*, rsh acts just like rlogin and starts a shell on the remote host.
`host`	Name of the remote computer.

You cannot run commands such as `vi` that require character-level interaction using rsh. If you wish to run such a command remotely, use rlogin.

When you use rsh, you have to be concerned about which machine — the local one or the remote one — is interpreting the commands:

♦ The local machine interprets shell metacharacters that are not quoted.

♦ The remote machine interprets quoted metacharacters.

For example, this command

`rsh tofu date > local.output`

executes the date command on the remote host (`tofu`) but saves the output in a file named `local.output` on your computer. However, this command

`rsh tofu date '>' remote.output`

executes `date` on the remote host and saves the output on the remote machine in a file named `remote.output`. Note that you can write this command as

`rsh tofu 'date > remote.output'`

Setting Up Your System to Use rlogin and rsh without Passwords

rlogin and rsh need to establish your real identity before they allow you to access a remote machine. The default configuration is to assume that you are attempting a remote login from a machine that may not be trusted. If you want to allow access without passwords, you need to configure the remote computer to accept the remote machine as being *equivalent* and that any login attempts are from the users that they claim to be. You can use either one of the following configurations:

✦ Establish system-wide configuration using the /etc/hosts.equiv file. This configuration applies to a single computer or, if the computer is on a network using NIS, it could be an entire network (*see* the NIS HowTo at www.linuxresources.com/LDP).

✦ Create your own personal configuration using the $HOME/.rhosts file which grants only you password-free access.

Using /etc/hosts.equiv

You use the /etc/hosts.equiv file to tell a computer system that any one of the named machines is equivalent in terms of permissions to itself. In other words, this file identifies machines trustworthy enough to be considered equivalent. Follow these steps to set up the /etc/hosts.equiv file:

1. Log in as **root**.

2. Edit /etc/hosts.equiv with your favorite editor (for example, use vi /etc/hosts.equiv). If the file does not already exist, the editor creates it.

3. Add a line with the name of the machine you trust to be equivalent. For example, if you are on machine tofu and you want to declare machine tempeh to be equivalent, just add a line with the word tempeh in it.

You really don't want to add a machine to your host equivalent file unless you are sure it can be trusted. Generally this means that you have administrative control over it.

Using .rhosts

.rhosts is a local file that allows each user to map between different accounts on different machines. Unlike the /etc/hosts.equiv file, which is global for everyone on the computer, .rhosts is unique for

each user. In these steps you are creating personal .rhosts files on all the machines you want to connect to.

1. Log in to each machine on which you want to establish a personal equivalence and create the file name .rhosts in your home directory.

2. Enter lines of the form `system userid` in this file for all the systems you want to enable equivalence. For example, if your login is `bill` on `whitehouse.gov` and `william` on `secret.net`, set up your .rhosts file like this:

```
whitehouse.gov bill
secret.net william
```

.rhosts has a drawback — it can present a significant security problem because it expands the possible ways people can log into your account.

telnet — Logging in Remotely

telnet is the most widely accepted method of logging in to a remote system. It is very much like a standard remote login you might do with a terminal emulator program, but telnet is designed to work over a TCP/IP connection.

LINUXspeak

`telnet [-e esc_char] [host] [port]`

Option or Argument	Function
`-e esc_char`	Sets the telnet escape character to esc_*char*. The default is normally Ctrl+].
`host`	Name of the remote computer.
`port`	The port number to use for the connection. The default is port 23. ***See*** /etc/services for a complete list of supported ports.

You can use telnet to check to see if other services are working. For example, you can telnet to port 25 to see if SMTP requests are being answered.

Connecting to the remote host using telnet

telnet acts much like a terminal emulator program that you might use to log onto a bulletin board system but it is designed to work over the Internet. Here's how to perform a remote login using telnet.

1. Type **telnet** and the name of the remote computer. telnet asks you for your login name.

2. Type your login name on the remote system and press Enter. telnet asks you for your password.

3. Enter your password (it won't be displayed as you type it) and press Enter. You should now be logged onto the remote system.

Sample

In this example, I telnet to biggie.fylz.com from smiley.fylz.com by typing telnet biggie.fylz.com. At the remote prompts, I enter my user i.d. and password.

```
Trying 198.186.207.131...
Connected to biggie.fylz.com.
Escape character is '^]'.

Linux 1.3.57 (biggie.fylz.com) (ttyp4)

biggie login: fyl
Password:
Last login: Sun Oct 5 13:48:51 from smiley.fylz.com
Linux 1.3.57.

biggie:~$
```

Terminating your telnet session

You can quickly terminate your telnet session by exiting the remote system the way you normally exit the remote system (by entering **exit** or **logout**, for example, if you are on a UNIX or LINUX system).

Here is the fail-safe way to exit telnet (even if the remote system is not currently responding):

1. Enter the telnet escape command (usually Ctrl+]).

2. At the telnet> prompt, type **close** to terminate the connection, or type **quit** to terminate the connection and exit telnet.

traceroute — *Finding the Route to a Remote Host*

Why is the Internet so slow? Why is your LAN so slow? Why can't you talk to a particular host? These are the sorts of questions traceroute is designed to answer.

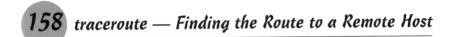

The traceroute program does its thing by sending ICMP (Internet Control Message Protocol) packets with small time-to-live values and the interpreting the responses to build a map of the path from your local machine to the distant host. The transmission of a packet from one host to another is called a *hop* and the time-to-live value is calculated in *hops*. For example, if the time-to-live value is ten, after the message has traveled (hopped) through ten hosts it's considered undeliverable. (I recommend sticking with the default settings listed in the table that follows.)

The Internet is a heterogeneous mix of computers. Not every computer or operating system handles these ICMP packets correctly. You may notice gaps or anomalies in the output of traceroute.

LINUXspeak

traceroute [-m *max*] [-n] [-q *qcount*] [-w *time*] *host*

Option or Argument	Function
-m *max*	Sets the maximum number of hops to attempt to reach the host. The default is 30.
-n	Prints the addresses of each machine along the path as a number rather than symbolically by host name. This saves the system from having to do a nameserver lookup in order to translate the IP address into a host name for each hop.
-q *qcount*	Sets the number of packets sent for each hop. The default is three.
-w *time*	Waits for *time* seconds for a response to a probe. The default is three seconds.
host	The remote machine that you want to trace the path to.

Sample

The following is the result of the command traceroute gw.ssc.com issued from my system at home. Each line represents a hop. The three individual times (in miliseconds) displayed for each hop are the times for each of the three queries.

```
traceroute to gw.ssc.com (199.184.169.1), 30 hops
    max, 40 byte packets
 1 max4.aa.net (204.157.220.29) 133.708 ms 138.532
    ms 159.407 ms
 2 r1/e0.aa.net (204.157.220.1) 139.231 ms 149.161
    ms 159.419 ms
 3 gw.ssc.com (199.184.169.1) 149.18 ms 179.139 ms
    179.441 ms
```

whois — Accessing DNS Registration Information

All nonmilitary domain names are registered with Internic, the organization that handles DNS (Domain Name Server) registrations (`rs.internic.net`). The registration information for each name includes the following:

- ✦ An IP address

- ✦ Contacts (names, e-mail addresses, and phone and fax numbers)

- ✦ The time of the last update

- ✦ Domain servers — computers that can be queried to translate your domain name into an IP address.

The Internic registration allows you to query by using any of the following:

- ✦ Domain name

- ✦ Handle (this is an ID made up by Internic)

- ✦ Contact name

If you want to register a new domain name, you can do so online. Just point your web browser at `rs.internic.net` and follow the directions under <u>registration services</u> link.

LINUXspeak

`whois` [`-h` *hostname*] *names*

Option or Argument	Function
`-h` *hostname*	Identifies the `whois` server to use. The default is `rs.internic.net`. Use `nic.ddn.mil` for sites in the `.mil` domain.
names	Specifies queries to send to the whois server.

Normally, the whois server searches all databases. If you want to restrict the search to a particular database, you can use one of the following query formats for *names*.

Format	What It Does
! *name*	Searches using *name* as a handle.
. *name*	Searches *name* database.
user@host	Does a look-up using the e-mail address database. Either *name* or *host* is optional. For example, *name@* finds all users whose name is *user* at any host.
AS	Searches for autonomous system number *name*.
DO *name*	Searches for domain *name*.
GA *name*	Searches for gateway *name*.
HO *name*	Searches for host *name*.
NE *name*	Searches for network *name*. *name* can also be a net number. For example, NE 204.157 finds all networks where the first two octets match 204.157.

If you type **whois help**, you receive detailed help from the whois server explaining all the possible options.

Sample

The following code chunk is the result of the query whois linuxjournal.com. Note that the strings in parenthesis (LINUXJOURNAL-DOM, PH43, and LB25) are the Internic handles for the domain and for two people. To restrict a query to a handle, use !*handle*.

```
[rs.internic.net]
Linux Journal Magazine (LINUXJOURNAL-DOM)
  PO Box 55549
  Seattle, WA 98155
  US

  Domain Name: LINUXJOURNAL.COM

  Administrative Contact:
  Hughes, Phil (PH43) fyl@SSC.COM
  206-782-7733
  Technical Contact, Zone Contact:
  Bahneman, Liem (LB25) roland@COBALTGROUP.COM
  (206) 957-7619

  Record last updated on 09-Apr-97.
  Record created on 13-Jan-94.
  Database last updated on 4-Oct-97 05:29:27 EDT.

  Domain servers in listed order:
```

```
UNCLE.SSC.COM              204.157.223.65
HENDRIX.AA.NET             204.157.220.4
BROKEDOWN.SSC.COM          204.157.223.78


The InterNIC Registration Services Host contains
    ONLY Internet Information (Networks, ASN's,
    Domains, and POC's).
Please use the whois server at nic.ddn.mil for
    MILNET Information.
```

## Part IX

Systems Administration

LINUX distributions offer a combination of high-level utilities to help you with systems administration. All in all, administering a LINUX system is not that much different from administering a UNIX system. So if you know how to administer UNIX, you may already be familiar with much of the information in this part of the book.

If your LINUX distribution has a GUI for systems administration, use it. If, however, something goes wrong, you may have to get down and dirty to fix it. (Which is why I take the time to cover the down-and-dirty part of systems administration.)

In this part . . .

- ✓ Adding users and groups
- ✓ Connecting to an ISP with PPP
- ✓ Starting and stopping the system
- ✓ Performing system maintenance
- ✓ Introducing kernel modules

Adding Users

You have a number of methods available to add a user. You can add a user by doing any of the following:

✦ Using the GUI supplied with your LINUX distribution

✦ Using the adduser command

✦ Making the necessary changes manually

The GUI and adduser command "hold your hand" while you add users. To add a user manually, you must be logged on as **root** and do all of the following things:

1. Edit /etc/passwd and add an entry for the new user.

2. If you are using shadow passwords, edit/etc/passwd and add an entry for the new user.

3. If the new user will have his or her own group, edit /etc/group and add a new group entry.

(For a description of the password file record format, the shadow password file record format, and the group file record format, *see* the "Managing User Control Files" section later in this part.)

4. Create the user's home directory using the mkdir command — for example, you can enter mkdir/home/newguy. (*See* Part III for more information.)

5. Change the ownership of the home directory to the new user — for example, you can enter chown newguy.users/home/newguy. (*See* Part III for more information.)

6. Copy any system default configuration files to the new user's home directory, making sure the ownership and permissions are correct.

7. Set the new user's password — for example, you can enter password newguy and follow the prompts.

Besides seeming like a lot of work, there are potential problems with this sequence. For example, someone else may be updating the password file while you are manually editing it. You are always better off to use the GUI or administration scripts to add users.

Checking File Systems

The `fsck` script runs the appropriate file system check program for each file system in /etc/mtab when the system is booted. A list of the programs that check the different file system types follows:

File System Type	Program
dosfsck	MS-DOS file system
e2fsck (or fsck.ext2)	Second extended file system (LINUX default)
fsck.minix	Minix file system
xfsck	Xia file system

The programs do a complete check if either of the following conditions exist.

+ The system was not properly shut down.

+ The file system has been mounted more times than the interval between checks as saved in the file system.

Follow these steps to manually check a file system:

1. Log on as root.

2. If possible, unmount the file system you are about to check (for example, you can enter umount/home).

3. To check and repair the filesystem, type fsck and the filesystem name and then press Enter. If you would rather have the program automatically perform the check without asking you to decide on the correct action, type fsck -a instead.

Deleting Users

Deleting users is pretty much the opposite of adding users. To delete a user, you must do the following:

1. Delete or change the owner of any files that belong to the user. (***See*** the find command in Part III for more information).

2. Delete the user from /etc/passwd.

3. If you are using shadow passwords, delete the user from /etc/shadow.

4. Delete the user from /etc/group. You may have to edit passwrd newguy multiple group file entries.

5. If the user's home directory is empty, delete it.

Finding System Files

You must use numerous files to maintain and administer the system. You can use the following shopping list to check off the files as you locate them.

File	Function
/etc/HOSTNAME	The name of your computer.
/etc/at.deny	A list of users who are not allowed to use the at command.
/etc/bashrc	Startup commands for the Bash shell.
/etc/crontab	A systemwide crontab file. It is much like the regular crontab files (**see** Part III) but also has a user name field.
/etc/exports	File system exports via NFS.
/etc/gettydefs	Serial line setup modes (for the getty process).
/etc/group	**See** "Managing User Control Files," later in this part.
/etc/hosts	Local file that offers a mapping from hostnames to IP addresses.
/etc/inittab	Run level control file. (**See** "Working with Run Levels" later in this part.)
/etc/issue	Text file that is displayed before the login prompt.
/etc/issue.net	Text file that is displayed before the login prompt for Internet connections.
/etc/ld.so.conf	Locations for the dynamic loader to look for run-time libraries.
/etc/motd	Text file that is displayed after you successfully log in.
/etc/mtab	Mount table for file systems.
/etc/passwd	Password file.
/etc/shadow	Shadow password file. Only used if shadow passwords are enabled.
/etc/syslog. conf	File to configure what system messages are logged and where they are logged.
/var/lock	Directory for lock files.
/var/log	Directory where all log files are kept.
/var/spool/ cron/crontabs	Crontab files for each user.
/var/spool/lpd	Directory for the print spooler. It contains control files as well as the print queues.
/var/spool/mail	Directory for incoming mail files.
/var/spool/ mqueue	Mail transfer agent (sendmail or smail) queue directory.

TIP

If you just want to know about recent important events on the system, you can type dmesg rather than looking through the files in /var/log. The command dmesg displays recent system messages.

Managing User Control Files

You identify users by creating entries for them in the password file. Each user also has an entry in the group and possibly in the shadow password file. (*See* the section on "Shadow passwords" on the next page.)

The group file

The /etc/group file shows which users have access to which groups. Each group has a line in the file. Each entry consists of four fields separated by colons.

Field	Meaning
1	Group name.
2	Group password. This is rarely used and very difficult to administer.
3	Group ID. This corresponds to field 4 of /etc/passwd.
4	A comma separated list of group members.

The following program shows a few lines from my /etc/group file. You can see that fyl, viki, george, john, and marsha are all members of the users group, whereas only fyl and viki are members of fyl group. User george has his own group.

```
root::0:root
bin::1:root,bin,daemon
users::100:fyl,viki,george,john,marsha
fyl::500:fyl,viki
george::501:george
```

The password file

The /etc/passwd file contains the password login information about all the users on the system. This is a text file with one line for each user. Each line contains seven fields separated by a colon.

Field	Meaning
1	Login name.
2	Encrypted password. If this field is empty, the user does not have a password. You can put an * in this field to disable this login.
3	User ID. The root login always has an ID of 0. Depending on your LINUX flavor, regular user IDs start somewhere between 100 and 1000.
4	Group ID. This establishes the default group for this login by associating it with an entry in the /etc/group file.
5	User name and other contact information.
6	Pathname of the user's home directory.
7	Pathname of the user's shell.

Coming up are a few more lines from my /etc/passwd file. Note that george doesn't have a password and root and fyl are the only other accounts that have valid passwords.

```
root:JVMFXsFvtOMQs:0:0:root:/root:/bin/bash
bin:*:1:1:bin:/bin:
daemon:*:2:2:daemon:/sbin:
fyl:Xpw.kT1c121ZY:1000:500:Phil Hughes:/home/fyl:/
    bin/bash
george::1001:501:George L. Tyrebyter:/home/george:/
    bin/bash
```

Shadow passwords

Some versions of LINUX (and UNIX) support *shadow passwords* that enhance security. The /etc/passwd file, which contains login information about all the users in the system, must be readable by everyone. When you use a shadow password, the password is moved from /etc/password to /etc/shadow and an x is placed in the password field of /etc/password. Permissions on /etc/shadow are set to prevent anyone except root from reading it.

Networking with PPP

PPP stands for *Point-to-Point protocol.* It is a common way to connect to an Internet service provider (ISP) using a dial-up connection over a standard phone line or ISDN line.

You need many pieces of properly configured software to make a successful PPP connection. Once you understand all those pieces, you should have little trouble getting PPP up and running on your system. (For more information on network addressing, **see** Part VIII.)

To get yourself connected, you need to follow these steps:

1. Dial the modem.

2. Log on to your ISP and start PPP.

3. Establish routing so that your data packets are sent over your PPP interface.

Once you have everything set up, you can do the whole sequence with one command.

To set up your PPP connection, you need to know these things:

+ The telephone number of your ISP.

+ The proper login sequence. This may involve standard LINUX-like logins or include other authorization requirements.

+ The IP addresses of the nameservers you are supposed to use.

+ The domain name of the machine you use as your mail server. You may notice two different addresses: one that a POP server uses to receive your mail and one that an SMTP server uses to send mail.

+ The name of the news server you use.

+ Your IP address if you have a static one. You probably do not have a static IP address unless you purchased dedicated service from your ISP. Having a static IP address for your PPP connection does not necessarily have to do with whether you have your own set of IP addresses — just how you need to talk to your ISP. For example, the address block 198.184.169.* belongs to me, but I still have a dynamic address assigned for the PPP connection each time I connect. My LINUX systems handle the routing from my addresses to the gateway to the ISP.

The following table lists example parameters I've used to set up a PPP connection. You may need to stick pop, mail, and news on the front of the ISP's domain name; check with your ISP first.

Parameter	*Value*
My ISP	aa.net
Telephone number	777-7777
Login sequence	LINUX-like with a login name and password
Name servers	204.157.220.4, 204.157.223.111
Mail server (POP)	pop.aa.net

(continued)

(continued)

Parameter	Value
Mail server (SMTP)	`mail.aa.net`
News server	`news.aa.net`
My IP address	dynamic

Once you have all this information, you have to decide what to do with it. If your LINUX distribution includes a GUI-based utility to set up a PPP, you probably have to fill out some forms with the information. Just enter the information, and you should be all set.

The chat program

chat establishes a dial-up connection. You can use another program such as dip, but chat is the best choice. For a more detailed look at this setup, *see Linux SECRETS* (IDG Books Worldwide, Inc.).

LINUXspeak

```
chat [-r rfile] [-t time] [-v] [-V] script
chat -f sfile [-r rfile] [-t time] [-v] [-V]
```

Option or Argument	Function
`-f sfile`	Reads the chat script from `sfile` rather than the command line.
`-r rfile`	Uses `rfile` as the report file. This is the location where chat writes strings from the REPORT script keyword. By default, chat writes these strings to standard error. (**See** Part II for more information.)
`-t time`	Waits *time* seconds for a reply.
`-v`	Logs all text received from the modem and output strings to the system log (usually /var/spool/messages).
`-V`	Sends all text received from the modem and output strings to standard error.
`script`	The actual chat script.

The chat script consists of a sequence of expect/send sequences. The first string tells chat what to expect to receive from the modem, and the second string tells chat what to send to the modem once it receives the expect sequence.

The expect sequence may also contain a subexpect/subsend sequence to deal with cases in which chat does not receive what it expected from the modem. You separate this sequence from the actual expect string with hyphens. For example, if you want an expect sequence that says wait for OK but send +++ and wait again if you don't get it, you would use

`'OK-+++\c-gin:'`

The \c tells chat not to send a Return character. By default, chat sends a Return character at the end of a send sequence but does not expect it at the end of an expect sequence.

You should only include enough information in the expect sequence so that chat can identify the sequence. For example, you can use gin: for login and word: for password. That way, even if the initial characters are garbled, chat recognizes the string.

chat recognizes the following special strings in what would normally be the expect field. (If one of these strings appears then it is configuration information to chat instead of an expect sequence.)

String	Result
ABORT	Aborts the connection attempt if the sequence following ABORT is received.
REPORT	Instructs chat to log information to the report file. If the string following the REPORT keyword matches a string being received from the modem, chat logs the matched string and all subsequent characters received from the modem until a control character is received.
TIMEOUT	Uses the value of the sequence following TIMEOUT as the number of seconds to wait on each expected string. The initial timeout is 45 seconds. You can use the TIMEOUT keyword multiple times in the script to change the timeout value for subsequent commands.

You can embed other special characters into a chat sequence (see the following table).

Chat Sequence	Result
^x	Functions as a control character for *x*. For example, to send an end of file character (Ctrl+D), type ^D in the send sequence.
BREAK	Sends a break sequence.
EOT	Sends Control+D.
' '	Expects or sends nothing.
\b	Backspace.
\c	Suppresses the newline at the end of a send string.
\d	Delays for one second.

(continued)

(continued)

Chat Sequence	Result
\K	Sends a break.
\n	Sends a Newline character.
\N	Sends a null character.
\p	Pauses for one-tenth of a second.
\q	Suppresses writing the string to the system log (useful for preventing passwords from being logged).
\r	Sends or expects a Return.
\s	Represents a space. (If you use \s instead of Space you do not have to quote the string.)
\t	Sends or expects a Tab.
\\	Sends or expects a backslash.
\ddd	Uses *ddd* as the octal value of a single character to send.

The first four lines of the following example specify conditions under which the connection attempt should be abandoned. The rest of the lines are expect/send sequences. The first item on the line tells chat what to expect from the remote computer, and the second item tells chat what to send. For example, the '' in Line 5 tells chat to expect nothing. Chat therefore immediately sends ATZ, which is the reset command to the modem.

All the subsequent lines tell chat to wait for the first string (OK, CONNECT, ogin:, and word:) and then send the second string. In the CONNECT line, the second string is ' ', so chat sends nothing and just continues on to the next line.

```
ABORT       BUSY
ABORT       'NO CARRIER'
ABORT       'NO DIALTONE'
ABORT       'Login incorrect'
''ATZ
OKATDT7777777
CONNECT     ''
ogin:       my_login_name
word:       my_password
```

Fixing the routing

When pppd has successfully completed *negotiation* (the setup sequence in which PPP establishes transmission parameters), it informs the kernel of the local and report IP addresses. (*See* "The ppd program" later in this part.) The kernel uses this information to add a host route to the remote end of the link.

✦ If you have specified to pppd the `defaultroute` option, pppd asks the kernel to add a default route to the routing table for this interface.

✦ If your machine is a gateway on a LAN, you probably should specify `proxyarp` in order to allow other hosts to communicate with the remote host. This option causes pppd to look for a network interface on the same subnet as the remote host. If found, pppd creates an ARP entry with the IP address of the remote host and the hardware address of the network interface it found.

✦ If you need to do something special once your connection is established, you can add commands to /etc/ppp/ip-up. This script is executed once the link is up.

✦ You can use the `ifconfig` and `route` commands.

Mail servers

If you use Post Office Protocol (POP) to retrieve messages, you need to tell the program you use to retrieve your e-mail about the POP server name. The program you use most likely is fetchmail. (*See* Part VI for more information on POP.)

If you send mail using SMTP, you probably want to send all your mail to a machine at your ISP that will forward it over the Internet. This machine is called your *smart host*. Without a smart host you would have to configure your local system to perform all the address lookups on the Internet and be responsible for mail forwarding to the final destination. Besides creating more work, your local machine would have to stay connected to the Internet until all the mail is delivered.

To configure your system for using a smart host, you need to give the name of the mail smart host to your mail transfer agent. If your MTA is sendmail, you need to assign the mail smart host name to the S macro in the sendmail.cf file. (For more information on configuring sendmail, *see* the *Network Administrators Guide* and Linux HowTo called *mail-HOWTO*. Both are available online from the LINUX Documentation Project. Most distributions include the HowTos on their CDs.)

If you send or receive mail with a Web browser such as Netscape or Internet Explorer, you need to include the names of your smart host as well as the name of your POP server in the browser's configuration options.

Making the connection

In order to establish a connection, you need to execute pppd with the right options. You can manually start the link by using a shell script. Just log on as root (or use su to become root) and run the script. The PPP code includes examples of a startup script (called ppp-on) and a shutdown script (called ppp-off). On Red Hat 4.2, these scripts are located in /usr/doc/ppp-2.2.0f-3/scripts. On other distributions, they may be incorporated into the standard startup scripts in /etc/rc.d or /etc/rc.d/init.d.

I used the sample script for pppd in the preceding section. I put the script in /usr/sbin and called it paa.

Rather than logging on as root each time you need to start or stop PPP, you can create logins for this task. For example, you can create a login named pppup to bring PPP up and one named pppdown to bring it down. By setting the user ID on these logins to 0, they run as root. Set their shells to the name of the script you want to run.

Name servers

You can list up to three nameservers in /etc/resolv.conf and you must list them by IP address. They are searched in the order they appear in the file. The following code snippet describes my /etc/resolv.conf file. The search line sets the default domain to fylz.com. This line instructs network applications to append fylz.com onto any address it receives that does not have a domain name before it attempts a DNS lookup. For example, if I use the e-mail address viki@smiley as a mail destination, the program performing the DNS lookup would append fylz.com to the address before performing the lookup.

```
search fylz.com
nameserver 204.157.220.4
nameserver 204.157.223.111
```

The News server

News readers are programs that allow you to read Usenet newsgroups, a collections of more than 20,000 different online discussion groups. Most newsreaders use the value of the NNTPSERVER environment variable in order to find the news server. To check to see if the variable is set properly, type echo $NNTPSERVER at your shell prompt.

Phone number and login sequence

Most systems place the files containing the phone number and login sequence in /etc/ppp. The Red Hat distribution places the files in /etc/sysconfig/network-scripts so that all the files accessed by their graphical network setup program are in the same directory. The chat program needs a file to use for instructions on how to make the connection. The file can be anywhere, as long as it is secure and the chat program knows where to find it. The file consists of some keyword instructions to chat and also the sequence to get the modem to talk, dial the phone number, and perform the login. *See* "The chat program," earlier in this part for a sample of this file.

If other people see your phone number and login sequence, then you have lost exclusive control over your ISP account. Make sure the permissions on these files do not allow access by any users other than root.

The pppd program

The pppd program handles the dial-up connection once it is established.

LINUXspeak

pppd [*tty*] [*speed*] [*options*]

Option or Argument	Function
tty	The device used to communicate with the modem. If you do not specify the device, pppd uses the *controlling terminal* (the device where you have entered the pppd command). You generally do not want pppd to use the controlling terminal unless you are very good at typing PPP packets. If you specify a device without a leading /dev, pppd will affix it.
speed	The baud rate to use for the link.
options	A set of options to define the operating characteristics of the link. These are in addition to the options specified in /etc/ppp/ options and $HOME/.ppprc. You can turn off Boolean options (such as crtscts) by preceding the keyword with a - (for example, -crtscts). If the default is off for an option, use +*option* to turn it on.

The following list contains additional pppd options. *See* the pppd man page (Section 8 of man) for a more complete list.

Option	Function
asyncmap *map*	Uses *map* to establish which control characters cannot be received over the serial line. This is a 32-bit bitmap specified in octal in which each bit represents a control character. Bit 0 (00000001) represents the character 0x00; bit 31 (8000000) represents the character 0x1F.
auth	Requires the peer to authenticate itself.
connect *cmd*	Uses the program or shell command specified to set up the serial connection. The invoking of chat appears here.
crtscts	Uses hardware (RTS/CTS) flow control.
defaultroute	Adds a default route to the system routing tables for this connection.
disconnect *cmd*	Runs *cmd* to disconnect the link after pppd has terminated.
escape *xx,yy,...*	Escapes the specified characters. You must put the values of the characters to be escaped in hexadecimal. (*Escaping* characters encapsulates them in a special sequence before sending them over the data link.)
file *optf*	Reads options from file *optf*.
lock	Creates a UUCP-style (Unix to Unix Communications Program) lock file to prevent other programs from accessing the device.
mru *n*	Sets the maximum receive unit value to *n* bytes.
mtu *n*	Sets the maximum transmit unit value to *n* bytes.
netmask *n*	Specifies a netmask for this interface. You must use dotted decimal notation (for example, 255.255.255.0).
silent	Doesn't send anything until the remote system sends a valid packet.
local:*remote*	Sets the local and/or remote interface IP addresses. You may omit either address. With dynamic addresses you generally don't need to specify either address. If you specify an address, pppd does not accept a different value unless you use the ipcp-accept-local or ipcp-accept-remote options.
bsdcomp *nr,nt*	Requests that the remote system compress packets use the BSD compress scheme. *nr* specifies the maximum code size in bits. Packets sent to the remote system are compressed with a maximum code size of *nt* bits. If you don't specify *nt*, *nt* defaults to the value of *nr*.

Option	Function
-bsdcomp	Turns off BSD compression.
+chap	Requires CHAP (Cryptographic Handshake Authentication Protocol) authentication.
-chap	Doesn't require CHAP.
debug	Increases the current debugging level.
detatch	Forks to become a background process.
dns-addr *ip*	Sets the IP address for the DNS server. Use it with Microsoft clients.
domain *d*	Appends the domain name *d* to the local host name for authentication purposes.
-ip	Disables IP address negotiation.
ipparam string	Sends this string as the sixth parameter to the ip-up and ip-down scripts.
kdebug *n*	Enables debugging code in the kernel-level PPP driver. This is an octal digit formed by adding 1 for general debugging messages, 2 for contents of received packets, and 4 for contents of sent packets.
login	Uses the system password database for authentication of a peer using PAP.
modem	Uses the modem control lines (default).
name *nam*	Sets the name of the local system to *nam* for authentication purposes.
+pap	Requires PAP authentication.
papcrypt	Specifies that the secrets in /etc/ppp/pap-secrets are encrypted.
proxyarp	Adds an entry to the local system's ARP (Address Resolution Protocol) table with the IP address of the remote system and the Ethernet address of this system.
remotename *nam*	Assumes the name of the remote system is *nam* for authentication purposes.
+ua *file*	Uses PAP for authentication if requested by the remote and uses the contents of the specified *file* for name and password.
usehostname	Enforces the use of the hostname as the name of the local system. This disallows the use of the name option.
user *u*	Sets the user name to *u* in order to use it for authentication with PAP.
xonxoff	Uses software flow control. Don't use this option unless you cannot use hardware flow control because it increases overhead and tends to be unreliable.

pppd looks for the options listed on the previous three pages in the following places:

✦ /etc/ppp/options

✦ .ppprc in your home directory

✦ On the command line

Authentication secrets are saved in

✦ /etc/ppp/pap-secrets for PAP

✦ /etc/ppp/chap-secrets for CHAP

Example

The following program is the connect script I use for my ISP:

```
/usr/sbin/pppd asyncmap 00000000 crtscts \
  modem lock defaultroute \
netmask 255.255.255.0 /dev/cual 57600 \
connect '/usr/sbin/chat -v -f /etc/ppp/ppp-aa'
```

I also have the following two program lines in my /etc/ppp/ip-up file, which is automatically executed after the PPP connection is established. This sets the maximum packet size on my PPP link to 296 characters (a good choice for slow links) and then executes a command to synchronize the clock on my computer to a clock that is known to be accurate. This file is also a good place to start fetchmail in order to automatically download your e-mail.

```
/sbin/ifconfig ppp0 mtu 296
~fyl/bin/rdate www.ssc.com
```

Setting Up Serial Ports for User Login

When the LINUX system is started, init uses the information in /etc/inittab to start programs on the consoles and serial ports that allow user logins. One program that is started is getty (or mgetty, a variant with additional options such as the ability to handle FAX connections). getty does the following:

✦ Opens the line and sets its modes, such as line speed.

✦ Waits for an indication of a login, gets the login name, and transfers control to the login program.

The two versions of getty use different configuration files:

✦ getty uses a file named /etc/default/getty.line to configure each individual line.

✦ mgetty uses files in the /etc/mgetty+sendfax directory, with
  mgetty.config being the main configuration file.

Shutting Down LINUX

As part of your systems administration duties, you may be called
upon to bring LINUX down in an orderly and secure way. To do so,
you must follow these steps:

1. Notify all logged-in users that the system is going down.

2. Block new logins.

3. Notify all programs that the system is going down (so they can
   do their cleanup).

LINUXspeak

```
shutdown [-h] [-r] time [message]
```

Option or Argument	Function
-h	Halts the system after shutdown.
-r	Reboots the system after shutdown (default).
time	When to perform the shutdown. This can be an absolute time specified as hh:mm, or a number of minutes to wait before performing the shutdown specified as +mins. The command now is a synonym for +0.
message	A message to send to all users.

Example

To shut down the system 5 minutes from now and notify users that
the system will be down for 30 minutes, you can type shutdown -
h +5 Back up in 30 minutes.

Each user would receive a message that looks like this:

```
Broadcast message from root (tty3) Wed Oct 8
   15:16:17 1997 ...
Back up in 30 minutes.
The system is going DOWN for system halt in 5
   minutes !!
```

Don't simply push reset or turn the power off to shut down the
system. LINUX buffers a lot of information (in order to run
efficiently). If you don't give LINUX a chance to do its cleanup,
your files may be damaged. The LINUX filesystem is extremely
good at recovering from such a powerdown, but that's no excuse
to risk damaging the system.

Starting LINUX

The way you configure LILO (the boot loader) when you install LINUX determines how the system starts up. You probably installed LILO in one of three modes:

+ Immediately boot LINUX.

+ Wait a predetermined amount of time (such as five seconds) and then boot some operating system.

+ Wait until a system ID is entered at the LILO prompt.

The following steps work no matter how you configure LILO.

1. When your computer is starting up, press and hold down the Shift key and wait for the LILO prompt.

2. Release the Shift key and press Tab. LILO displays a list of boot choices (such as DOS, LINUX, or whatever you decided to type in when you configured LILO).

3. Type in your selection and press Enter. LILO locates and loads the system you chose.

If you have just booted LINUX and want to go back and check the startup messages, you can page through the messages with Shift+PageUp and Shift+PageDown.

Using the cron Program

The cron program is started at boot time and runs every minute. cron then runs any jobs that are scheduled to run at the current time. The scheduled jobs are in either /etc/crontab (the system crontab file) or in files whose names are the individual user names in the /var/spool/cron/crontabs directory.

To change the system crontab file, you only need to edit the file and make the desired modifications. The cron program checks the file each time it runs. You can modify individual crontab files by using the crontab program. (***See*** Part III for more on crontab.)

Working with Run Levels

Run levels allow the system to be configured in many different ways without having to modify configuration files. Each run level represents a particular configuration. For example, you might want to have one run level for your system running alone and another for your system connected to a network (local, PPP link, or both).

LINUX is a multi-tasking system. In normal operation, lots of processes, called *daemons,* run in the background to support the system users. Examples of some daemons are init, which sets up the multi-user environment; network daemons that handle NFS; telnet and rlogin requests; sendmail, which queues and sends mail; and the print spooler, which manages the print queues and delivers work to the printers. Because daemons are at work, you must stop them in an orderly fashion before shutting off your computer.

Adding a new start or kill file

If you want to add something totally new to the init system, just follow these steps:

1. Write a start and a kill script.

2. Place the scripts in the init.d directory.

3. Add links to them in the directory where you want them to be executed. Use a name that starts with S for startup, or K for kill.

4. Type telinit q to get init to reread the script files.

Changing run levels

You use the /sbin/telinit program (which is generally just a link to /sbin/init) to change run levels. When the system boots, init starts with the run level specified in the entry in /etc/inittab that has an action of initdefault. Follow these steps if you want to change run levels:

1. Log in as root.

2. Type telinit followed by the desired run level (0 through 6).

  • If you have edited /etc/inittab or any of the script files and want init to re-read the files, type telinit q.

  • To switch to single user mode, type telinit s.

Not all LINUX distributions use the same run-level definitions; however, run levels 0, 1, and 6 are the same in Caldera, Debian, Red Hat, and Slackware. Run levels 2 through 5 are always multiuser but their specific use varies.

Run Level	Use
0	System shutdown
1	Single user mode
2	Multiuser without networking (Red Hat)
3	Full multiuser (Red Hat)
4	Multiuser running X only (Slackware)
5	Multiuser (Slackware); multiuser with X (Red Hat)
6	Reboot

Example inittab file

The easiest way to understand /etc/inittab is to look at a sample file. The following example includes explanatory comments (which start with #).

```
# /etc/inittab: init(8) configuration.
# The default runlevel.
id:2:initdefault:

# Boot-time system configuration/initialization
    script.
# This is run first except when booting in emer-
    gency
# (-b) mode.
si::sysinit:/etc/init.d/boot

# What to do in single-user mode.
~~:S:wait:/sbin/sulogin

# /etc/init.d executes the S and K scripts upon
    change
# of runlevel.
#
# Runlevel 0 is halt.
# Runlevel 1 is single-user.
# Runlevels 2-5 are multi-user.
# Runlevel 6 is reboot.

l0:0:wait:/etc/init.d/rc 0
l1:1:wait:/etc/init.d/rc 1
l2:2:wait:/etc/init.d/rc 2
l3:3:wait:/etc/init.d/rc 3
l4:4:wait:/etc/init.d/rc 4
l5:5:wait:/etc/init.d/rc 5
l6:6:wait:/etc/init.d/rc 6

# What to do when CTRL-ALT-DEL is pressed.
ca:12345:ctrlaltdel:/sbin/shutdown -t1 -r now
```

```
# What to do when the power fails/returns.
pf::powerwait:/etc/init.d/powerfail start
pn::powerfailnow:/etc/init.d/powerfail now
po::powerokwait:/etc/init.d/powerfail stop

# /sbin/getty invocations for the runlevels.
#
# The "id" field MUST be the same as the last
# characters of the device (after "tty").
#
# Format:
# <id>:<runlevels>:<action>:<process>
1:2345:respawn:/sbin/getty 38400 tty1
2:23:respawn:/sbin/getty 38400 tty2
3:23:respawn:/sbin/getty 38400 tty3
4:23:respawn:/sbin/getty 38400 tty4
5:23:respawn:/sbin/getty 38400 tty5
6:23:respawn:/sbin/getty 38400 tty6

# Example how to put a getty on a serial line
# (for a terminal)
#
#T1:23:respawn:/sbin/getty -L ttyS1 19200 vt100

# Example how to put a getty on a modem line.
#
#T3:23:respawn:/sbin/mgetty -x0 -s 57600 ttyS3
```

Setting up files in the run level directories

The init program handles run level changes. When that happens, init will

♦ Execute all the scripts in the directory of the old run level that start with the letter K. init executes scripts in the order they are displayed in the output of the ls command.

♦ Execute all the scripts in the directory of the new run level that start with the letter S. init executes scripts in the order they are displayed in the output of the ls command.

For example, assume you are in run level 2 and you are going to run level 3. Also assume the files in the rc2.d directory are K10_undoit, S10_doit, and S20_startgoodstuff, and that the files in the rc3.d directory are K10_nfs, K20_rpc, K30_zap, S10_nfs, S20_rpc, and S40_greet. init executes rc2.d/K10_undoit, rc3.d/S10_nfs, rc3.d/S20_rpc, and finally rc3.d/S40_greet.

System run levels

When you start LINUX, various programs need to be started. In order to make the program selection configurable, there exists a file called /etc/inittab and a set of directories containing startup scripts or programs. On Red Hat, these directories are in the /etc/rc.d directory. On Debian, they are in /etc. While there is some room for variability between LINUX flavors, the following table provides you with the general structure.

Filename	Function
init.d	Master directory of all the startup files. Each run level directory links back to the files in this directory.
rc	Initial startup file. It is also executed when the run level is changed. On Debian, a directory named rc.boot contains startup files.
rc0.d	Directory of files to run at runlevel 0.
rc1.d	Directory of files to run at runlevel 1.
rc2.d	Directory of files to run at runlevel 2.
rc3.d	Directory of files to run at runlevel 3.
rc4.d	Directory of files to run at runlevel 4.
rc5.d	Directory of files to run at runlevel 5.
rc6.d	Directory of files to run at runlevel 6.
rc.local	Local configuration file.
rc.sysinit	File that is run at boot time. (Red Hat only.)

The run level scheme just described was derived from UNIX System V. Some earlier LINUX distributions don't use it. They use a system based on Berkeley UNIX that has files instead of directories for each run level. The files have names such as rc.1, rc.2 and so on. The basic concept is the same, but you have to edit multiple files to make a change that affects multiple run levels.

Along with the run levels and directories, the /etc/inittab file controls the system action at each run level. Each line in this file is a sequence of commands separated by colons with entries in the following format:

id:*runlevels*:*action*:*process*

The fields are defined as shown in the table on the following page:

Field	Function
id	A one- to four-character identifier that uniquely identifies the line.
runlevel	A string of digits that identifies the run levels where this entry is to be activated. For example, the string 235 means this entry is to be activated at run levels 2, 3, and 5.
action	The action to take with regard to this entry (**see** the following table).
process	The process to be executed.

The following lists valid choices for action.

Keyword	Meaning
boot	Executes the process during the system boot. The *runlevel* field is ignored.
bootwait	Executes the process during the system boot and waits for it to complete before continuing the boot process. The *runlevel* field is ignored.
ctrlaltdel	Executes the process when Ctrl+Alt+Del is pressed on the system console.
initdefault	Specifies the default run level in the *runlevel* field.
kbrequest	Executes when a special keyboard sequence is received (still under development).
off	This entry is ignored by init.
once	Runs once when the specified run level is entered.
ondemand	Runs when an ondemand run level is called (but no run level change is made). The ondemand run levels are a, b, and c.
powerfail	Starts this process when a power failure signal is received.
powerwait	Executes the process when a power failure signal is received; init waits for this process to be completed.
powerokwait	Executes the process when the power ok (SIGPWR) signal is received.
respawn	Starts a process and restarts it whenever it terminates. Programmers commonly use it for the getty processes that make logins possible on the consoles and serial ports.
sysinit	Runs at boot time before any boot or bootwait entries. The *runlevel* field is ignored.
wait	The process is executed when the run level is entered, and init waits for its completion.

## Part X

Using Regular Expressions

Regular expressions provide a way to quickly and concisely specify the criteria for matching or selecting a string of characters. (I could have probably filled an entire Quick Reference on regular expressions, but I had a feeling my editor wouldn't let me.)

You can use regular expressions for pattern matching in awk, ed, egrep, fgrep, grep, sed, and vi for starters. You can also call regular expression matching tools from C programs. Once you understand the basics in this part, you are well on your way to becoming a regular expression guru.

In this part . . .

- ✔ **Understanding simple regular expressions**
- ✔ **Combining regular expressions**
- ✔ **Looking at some examples**

Examining Simple Regular Expressions

The regular expression matching mechanism attempts to find the longest match for the specified regular expression. A string of characters is the simplest regular expression. It matches one string, that being itself.

You can add the expressions in the table that follows to expand upon what is matched. Simple expressions can also be combined to create more complex expressions such as the ones in the next section.

Expression	Meaning
c	Says that any character except the special characters / ( ) * . | + ? [^ $\ matches itself
\c	Matches special character c
\nnn	Matches char with ASCII value nnn octal (base 8)
.	Matches any single character except a Newline
[list]	Matches any character in list where list is one or more single chars or ranges specified with -
[^list]	Matches any char not in list
^	Anchors pattern match to start of string
$	Anchors pattern match to end of string

Combining Simple Regular Expressions

When using a regular expression, the goal is to build one that matches what you are searching for or substituting. To build a more complicated regular expression, you can combine simple regular expressions. For example, the regular expression [0-9] matches a single digit. If you need to match a series of digits, adding a + to the simple expression turns it into a match for one or more digits.

Combination	Meaning
(re1)(re2)	Matches regular expression re1 concatenated with regular expression re2
re*	Matches 0 or more occurrences of the regular expression
re+	Matches 1 or more occurrences of the regular expression
re?	Matches 0 or 1 occurrences of the regular expression
re1|re2	Matches regular expression re1 or regular expression re2
(re)	Matches the regular expression
( )	Ensures precedence of the expression — optional

Samples of Basic Regular Expressions

Armed with the information in the previous two tables, I present you with some sample regular expressions so you can put the theory into practice. The following table lists regular expressions and what they match.

Regular Expression	Matches
d?g	Any three-letter string that starts with d and ends with g.
^From	Any string that begins with From.
^$	An empty line.
^X*YZ	Any line that begins with 0 or more of the character X followed by YZ. To ensure at least one X, use ^XX*YZ or ^X+YZ.
^....m	Any string that has an m as the fifth character.
[a-z]+	Any string of one or more lowercase letters.
[^aA]	Any string that does not begin with a or A.

Online Resources

You can find plenty of information about the LINUX operating system on the Internet. You can download versions of LINUX distributions, read on-line magazines about LINUX, participate in user newsgroups, and much more.

Try the list of resources in this part or click the <u>GLUE</u> link at www.LINUXresources.com to search for a user group in your area.

General Web Resources

The following Web sites offer extensive information on LINUX:

sunsite.unc.edu/LDP — This is the location of the LINUX Documentation Project pages.

www.LINUXresources.com — This is a general information site with emphasis on the business and professional aspects of LINUX. It has links to most other LINUX information sites as well as to its own individual content, which includes employment ads, a speaker's bureau, and GLUE (a LINUX user group directory).

Distribution Web Pages

Each LINUX vendor maintains its own Web site. Many of these vendor sites contain mirrors (copies) of other LINUX information. The Debian, Red Hat, and Slackware sites include complete downloadable versions of their distributions. Cruise to the following sites for more distribution information:

www.caldera.com — Caldera distribution

www.cdrom.com — Official Slackware distribution

www.craftwork.com — Craftwork LINUX distribution

www.infomagic.com — LINUX mirror, commercial CD sales

www.pht.com — LINUX mirror, commercial CD sales

www.suse.com — S.U.S.E. LINUX distribution

www.redhat.com — Red Hat distribution

FTP Resources

The following FTP (File Transfer Protocol) sites offer information on LINUX from public archives all over the Net:

tsx-11.mit.edu/pub/LINUX — General LINUX archive site

ftp.cdrom.com/pub/LINUX — Official home of Slackware

ftp.debian.org — Official home of Debian

ftp.caldera.com/pub/OpenLINUX — LINUX archive, Caldera patches

sunsite.unc.edu/pub/LINUX — General LINUX archive site

Magazines

In addition to the following magazines published in English, *LINUX Journal* is translated into Japanese, Korean, and Polish.

www.LINUXjournal.com — Monthly magazine published in the United States.

www.LINUXgazette.com — Monthly online LINUX magazine. You can read the magazine online or download it and read it at your leisure.

Usenet Newsgroups

A whole host of online newsgroups gather to discuss LINUX. Some of the groups are moderated, which means they have specific requirements and the content must pass muster with a moderator, but most of the groups welcome general postings. The following list provides names of newsgroups and the general topics under discussion.

alt.os.LINUX.caldera — Postings specific to the Caldera LINUX distribution

comp.os.LINUX.advocac — Benefits of LINUX compared with other operating systems

comp.os.LINUX.alpha — LINUX on Digital Alpha machines

comp.os.LINUX.announce — Announcements important to the LINUX community (moderated)

comp.os.LINUX.answers — FAQs, HOWTOs, READMEs, and other information about LINUX (moderated)

comp.os.LINUX.development.apps — Writing LINUX applications; porting to LINUX

comp.os.LINUX.development.system — LINUX kernels, device drivers, and modules

comp.os.LINUX.hardware — Hardware compatibility with the LINUX operating system

comp.os.LINUX.m68k — LINUX operating system on 680x0 Amiga, Atari, VME

comp.os.LINUX.misc — LINUX-specific topics not covered by other groups

comp.os.LINUX.networking — Networking and communications under LINUX `comp.os.LINUX.powerpc` — LINUX systems running on PowerPC microprocessors

`comp.os.LINUX.setup` — LINUX installation and system administration

`comp.os.LINUX.x` — LINUX X Window System servers, clients, libs, and fonts

`LINUX.debian.announce` — Announcements about Debian LINUX

`LINUX.redhat.install` — Discussions and help on installing Red Hat LINUX

Techie Talk

absolute pathname: The location of a file relative to the top of the file hierarchy. Also knows as a full pathname; an absolute pathname starts with a / (slash).

alias: A synonym. Aliases exist within the shell as abbreviations for commands and in e-mail as shorthand for mail addresses.

argument: A command line parameter passed to a program. Also, what you get when you mention vi to an Emacs junkie or Emacs to a vi junkie.

ARP: Address Resolution Protocol. This protocol maps IP addresses to hardware addresses.

ASCII (American Standard Code for Information Interchange): The standard code used for storing characters, including control characters on computers.

background: Running a program without it maintaining control of the terminal device. You start a program in the background by appending an ampersand (&) to the command line that invokes it.

BASH (Born Again SHell): The shell developed by the Free Software Foundation that is upward compatible with the UNIX System V (Bourne) Shell.

bin: The name of one of many program directories. /bin and /usr/bin exist on all systems. You may also have your own bin directory.

CHAP (Challenge/Handshake Authentication Protocol): One of the two popular protocols used by PPP for authentication. PAP is the other.

client-server: In X, the client program does the work and the server interacts with the user.

command interpreter: A shell. The program that reads and interprets user input.

command mode: In vi, the mode in which all key functions are commands rather than text entries.

compression: A way to shrink files or decrease the number of characters sent over a communications connection. File compression programs include compress, zip, and gzip.

csh: Pronounced *cee-shell,* csh is a shell developed by Bill Joy at the University of California at Berkeley. csh was the first UNIX shell to offer command history and substitution, a feature that is now available in the Bash and Korn shells.

CTS (Clear To Send): The control signal on a serial interface that tells the computer that the modem is ready to send data.

daemon: A program that runs in the background and performs various tasks. Examples include sendmail, which delivers e-mail, and lpd, which handles the print queues.

desktop: A graphical work environment. It includes a screen background, possibly a task bar, and an assortment of icons.

distribution: One of several LINUX products. A distribution consists of LINUX software, installation programs, and possibly proprietary software.

DNS (Domain Name System): The hierarchical method used to organize host names.

dvi (DeVice Independent): A intermediate file format used by troff, LaTeX, and other formatting software. You can convert dvi files into various output formats with utility programs.

filter: A program that can read from standard input and write to standard output.

flag: An option. Flags are relics from UNIX Version 6, and therefore they differ from today's options in that they do not have a - (hyphen) in front of them. ar and tar are two programs that still use flags.

fork: What LINUX uses to create a new process. The fork operation makes a clone of the current process.

FVWM (Feeble Virtual Window Manager): The most popular window manager used with the X window system.

GNU: Stands for GNU's Not Unix. GNU is an attempt by the Free Software Foundation to write a UNIX-like operating system called the Hurd. While the Hurd remains incomplete, LINUX has drawn heavily on its utilities, including gcc, the GNU C compiler.

GPL (GNU Public License): A software licensing agreement developed at the Free Software Foundation to insure that free software remains free. Most of LINUX is covered by the GPL.

GUI (Graphical User Interface): An interface that allows you to use your computer by pointing at objects with a mouse and clicking instead of typing in commands.

hidden file: A file having a name starting with a dot (.). Use the -a option on the ls command to see hidden files.

home directory: The directory you are in when you first log in. It is specified in your password file entry and is usually a subdirectory of /home.

host: A computer. Commonly used when talking about computers connected on a network.

I/O redirection: *See* redirection.

inode: An entry in a file system in which all information about a file (except its name) is stored.

insert mode: In vi, the mode in which you enter text.

Internet: A huge network of networks connecting computers globally.

IP (Internet Protocol): The protocol used for addressing messages on the Internet and some local networks.

ISDN (Integrated System Digital Network): A digital network offering higher speed connections than conventional POTS (plain old telephone service).

kernel: The guts of the operating system. The kernel is responsible for allocating resources and protecting users from one another.

kill: To terminate a process. Various kinds of kill commands send different signals to the process being terminated.

Korn shell: The shell developed by David Korn at AT&T. It is upward compatible with the Bourne shell. You can buy it for use with LINUX, or you can obtain a freeware clone called pdksh.

LILO (LINUX LOader): The boot loader than comes with LINUX. You can use it to boot multiple operating systems including those from Microsoft.

link: An additional name for a file. You create links using the ln command.

login directory: *See* home directory.

man (manual) page: A highly technical description of a file or command. The man command reads one of these guys.

Meta key: A special key such as the Control key used by Emacs for additional control functions. If your keyboard has an Alt key, it acts as the Meta key. If you do not have an Alt key, press Esc and then the key that was to be associated with the Meta key.

MIME (Multipurpose Internet Mail Extensions): A means to attach any type of file, including multimedia, to an e-mail message.

mount: To attach a new file system to an existing directory.

NFS (Network File System): A networking system that allows you to share files between computers. NFS was developed by Sun Microsystems and is available for virtually all UNIX implementations as well as for LINUX.

NIS (Network Information System): Originally called yellow pages, NIS allows you to share password files, machine names, and other files in a consistent manner.

option: A special kind of argument sent to a command. Options start with a hyphen.

PAP (Password Authentication Protocol): One of the two popular protocols used by PPP for authentication. CHAP is the other.

parent directory: The directory that contains the current directory.

partitioning: Dividing an allocatable device (such as a hard drive) into a number of pieces.

permissions: A set of bits that identify who has the right to read, write, or execute a file. For directories, the permissions identify who can read, write, or search.

pipe: A connection (entered using the | character) between the output of the program to the left of the pipe and the input of the program to the right of the pipe.

POP (Post Office Protocol): The common protocol used for downloading mail from an ISP.

POSIX: The IEEE standard for a portable operating system. The POSIX standard was derived from UNIX. LINUX complies with this standard.

PostScript: A computer language designed specifically to describe printable and displayable pages. Many high-end printers interpret PostScript.

PPP (Point to Point Protocol): Protocol used to send data over serial lines. Although commonly used to send IP packets, you can use PPP with other protocols such as Novell's IPX.

process: A running program.

prompt: A string of characters displayed by the shell or a program to identify that it is waiting for user input.

redirection: To alter the destination of the input or output of a program.

Regular Expression: A pattern-matching mechanism used by many UNIX and LINUX utility programs.

root: The login name for a super user.

root directory: The top level directory in a file hierarchy.

route: The path between one machine and another. Commonly used in networking.

RTS (Request to Send): The control signal on a serial interface that tells the modem that the computer wants to send data.

screen editor: A text editor that displays a window into a file rather than displaying text on a line-by-line basis. Emacs, joe, pico, and vi are all examples of screen editors. Screen editors are commonly used to write program files and edit text that will be processed by a text formatter such as LaTeX or troff.

script: *See* shell script. awk and Perl programs are traditionally called scripts.

search path: A list of directories, typically stored in your $PATH environment variable, in which the shell looks for executable programs.

server: The part of the X window system that is responsible for displaying information.

shell: The command interpreter that interacts with the user.

shell script: A program written in the language of the shell.

SMTP (Simple Mail Transfer Protocol): The common protocol for transferring electronic mail. Mail Transfer Agents such as sendmail use SMTP.

super user: The user/administrator who has access to everything in a system.

symbolic link: Also known as a *soft link,* a symbolic link is a pointer from a filename to the location of a file.

system administrator: The person responsible for keeping the computer system running.

TCP (Transmission Control Protocol): The most common reliable protocol that uses IP to transfer messages. TCP adds the necessary checks on top of IP to make sure a message is delivered.

Telnet: A program that enables you to remotely log into a computer system.

text formatter: A program that interprets special control sequences in text files and produces fancy-looking documents. LaTeX and groff are examples of such programs.

tcsh: An enhanced version of csh that offers file name completion and a built-in vi and Emacs-like editor.

Usenet: The Net before the Internet. Today, Usenet remains the source of newsgroups.

user name: The name you use to identify yourself to your LINUX system.

utility: A program that comes with LINUX or has been added to LINUX to perform a task.

UUCP (UNIX to UNIX Communications Program): A batch-oriented method of transferring e-mail and news files over phone lines.

uuencoded file: A binary file that has been translated into coded ASCII text. uuencoding is used to transmit non-text information via e-mail.

vi: Pronounced *vee-eye* by 70 percent of the people, *vi* (like violet) by 29 percent of the people, and *six* by the other 1 percent. One of two UNIX-based editors. Emacs is the other.

virtual memory: The memory you pretend you have but don't really have. On systems that support virtual memory, you can use as much memory as you want and the operating system uses swap space on the disk for the missing memory.

wildcard: A special character that tells the shell to look for a match from available file names. ? matches a single character, and * matches 0 or more characters.

window manager: A program that allows you to manipulate windows by moving, resizing, or closing them.

working directory: Your current directory. Type **pwd** to find out what it is.

X server: The part of the X window system that is responsible for displaying the information.

X window system (or just X): A GUI designed at the Massachusetts Institute of Technology. X is the de facto GUI standard for UNIX and LINUX.

zsh: A shell similar in function to the Korn shell (ksh).

Index

A

absolute pathname, 195
Accelerated X, 76–77
adduser command, 164
alias command, 16–17, 195
Allen, Joseph H., 96
anonymous FTP servers, 143–144
  ncftp, 144
  /pub directory, 147
applications, starting, 92
Applications menu, 83–84
applications windows, 77–78
Applixware, 95
appointment calendar, 80
archive CDs, 8
archive files, 30–32
arguments, 195
ARP (Address Resolution Protocol), 195
asc command, 148
ASCII (American Standard Code of
  Information Interchange), 195
ASCII encoding, 35–36
at command, 37–38

B

background, 195
backslash (and character quoting, 14–15
Badros, Greg J., 76
BASH (Bourne Again SHell), 14, 195
  command history, 15–16
  environment variables, 25
  setting editing modes, 18–19
  setting shell variables to environment
    variables, 25
  setup file and startup files, 27
bin, 195
Bourne, Stephen, 14
BSD UNIX, 6
button bars, 93

C

cal command, 38–39
Caldera, 7
Caldera Web site, 192
calendar, displaying, 38–39
cat command, 40–41
cd command, 14, 60–61, 145, 147, 148

CD-ROM, unable to mount, 11
CHAP (Challenge/Handshake
  Authentication), 195
character count, 68
character quoting, 14–15
chat program, 170–172
chgrp command, 56
chmod command, 57–58
chown command, 59
click-to-focus method, 78
client, 76
client-server, 196
closing windows, 89
cmp, 33
command history, 15–16
command interpreter, 13, 196
command line environment, 75
command mode, 196
commands
  arguments, 25
  command line options, 25
  connecting, 21–22
  directory management, 14
  executing within back quotes, 15
  making up names for, 16
  redirecting input and redirecting
    output, 22
  reexecuting, 15
  running in background, 79
compression, 196
configuration files, 27
Conroy, Dave G., 100
cp command, 42
cpio command, 30–32
Craftwork LINUX Web site, 192
creation mask, 59–60
cron program, 180
crontab command, 39–40
csh, 196
CTS (Clear To Send), 196
customizing environment, 16–20

D

daemons, 181, 196
dash and double dash conventions, 42
Debian LINUX, 7
Debian Web site, 192
decoding ASCII encoding, 35–36

decompressing and comparing files, 33
decompressing and displaying files, 33
decompressing and searching for
     patterns with grep, 33
desk calculator, 80
desktop, 196
destroying windows, 89
df command, 61
diff command, 24, 33
dir command, 145, 147
directories
     changing, 14, 60–61
     copying, 42
     creation, 62–63
     displaying current location, 63
     free disk space, 61
     identifying, 14
     management commands, 14
     naming conventions, 20
     new, 14
     removing empty, 14, 63
     used disk space, 61–62
directory referencing, 20
disk space, 61–62
DISPLAY environment variable, 19
distributions, 196
     differences in, 7–8
     Web sites, 192
dmesg command, 167
DNS (Domain Name Server), 159, 196
documentation, 46–48
domain names, 122
     registering, 159
domains, 142
dotted quad notation, 142
double quotes (") string quoting, 15
du command, 61–62
dvi (DeVice Independent), 196

E

echo command, 17
editing text
     Emacs, 102–104
     joe (Joe's Own Editor), 96–99
     Pico, 100–101
     vi, 104–114
elm, 120
     commands, 126
     exiting, 123–124
     Expert user level, 122
     help, 124
     mail aliases, 122–123
     mail management, 122–127

options, 127
pine and, 129
printing messages, 124
reading from another file, 125
reading messages, 124–125
saving messages, 125
sending messages, 126
tagging messages, 126–127
Emacs, 96
     commands, 102–103
     editing commands, 19
     editing text, 102–104
     environment of, 96
     exiting, 103
     starting, 104
Emacs mode, 15, 18–19
e-mail, 119
     attachments, 129
     displaying attachment contents, 120
     dissecting addresses, 121–122
     elm, 120, 122–127
     mail retrieval protocol choices, 130
     mail servers, 173
     metamail attachments, 127
     MIME (Multipurpose Internet Mail
          Extensions) messages, 120–121
     MTAs (mail transfer agent), 120
     MUA (mail user agent), 120
     pine, 120, 127–129
     POP (Post Office Protocol), 120, 129
     PPP (Point-to-Point Protocol), 120
     printing messages, 124, 128
     programs necessary for, 120
     reading messages, 124–125, 128
     remote access, 129–130
     saving messages, 125, 128
     sending messages, 126, 128–129
     sendmail, 120
     smail, 120
     smart host, 173
     SMTP (Simple Mail Transfer
          Protocol), 120
     tagging messages, 126–127
e-mail addresses, 121–122
environment variables, 17
     displaying, 17
     setting, 17–18
     setting shell variables to, 25
     standard, 19–20
error messages, redirecting, 23
exit command, 68–69
export command, 17, 18

F

fetchmail, 129–130, 173
file command, 63–64
file management basics, 40–48
  copying files and directories, 42
  dash and double-dash conventions, 42
  displaying contents, 40–41
  displaying filenames and information,
    43–44
  moving files, 45
  paging through files, 43
file manipulation, 30–37
  archive file creation, 30–32
  ASCII encoding, 34–35
  compressing and decompressing files,
    32–33
  decoding ASCII encoding, 35–36
  decompressing and comparing files
    using, 33
  decompressing and displaying files, 33
  decompressing and searching for
    patterns using grep, 33
  listing files without decompressing, 36
  restoring archive files, 30–32
  tar archives, 33–34
  unzip archives, 36–37
  uuencoding, 34–35
  zip archives, 36–37
file system check, 165
filenames
  case-sensitivity, 23
  displaying information, 43–44
files
  associated with program, 21–23
  comparing, 55–56
  compressing, 32–33
  copying, 42
  creation mask, 59–60
  decompressing, 32–33
  deletion, 66–67
  describing contents, 63–64
  displaying contents, 40–41
  finding quickly, 54–55
  first part, 64–65
  group, 56
  last part, 67
  locating, 52–53
  merging, 55–56
  moving, 45
  multiple names, 65–66
  naming conventions, 23
  ownership, 59
  paging through, 43

  pathnames, 23
  patterns within, 53–54
  permissions, 57–58
  print formatted, 51
  redirecting, 21
  sorting, 55–56
filesystems, mounting, 70–71
filters, 21–22, 196
find command, 52–53
finger command, 69–70
FIPS (First Interactive Partitioning
    System), 9
flag, 196
fmt command, 64
  vi and, 114
focus, 78
focus-follows-mouse method, 78
fork, 196
formatting text, 114–116
fsck script, 165
ftp command, 143, 144
FTP (file transfer protocol), 143–148
FVWM95
  configuration, 76
  focus styles, 78
  iconifying windows, 89
  sloppy focus method, 78
FVWM (Feeble Virtual Window Manager),
    75, 76, 196
  applications windows, 77–78
  miniature view of desktops, 78
  Pager, 77, 78
  root window, 79
  Task Bar, 79
  virtual desktops, 77–79
  virtual size, 77
  xload, 78

G

Games menu, 84
general LINUX archive site, 192
getty program, 178–179
GhostScript, 80
Ghostview, 80
GNU, 196
GNU-style documentation, 46
GPL (GNU Public License), 197
graphical environment, 75
graphics, 82
grep command, 22, 53–54
  looking in files for Content-Type:
    lines, 121

groff, 95
  commands in text files, 115
  filters, 115
  formatting text, 114–116
  macro packages, 115
  man pages, 116
  table, equation, and picture preprocessors, 115
GUI (Graphical User Interface), 164, 197
gv command, 48–49, 80
gzip command, 32–33

H

hard drives, 9
hardware problems, 11–12
hash command, 148
hash tables, 117
hcd command, 138
hcopy command, 138
hdel command, 138–139
hdir command, 139
head command, 64–65
hidden file, 197
history command, 15
HISTSIZE shell variable, 15
hmkdir command, 139
hmount command, 137, 139
home directory, 197
HOME environment variable, 19
HOME shell variable, 26
hops, 158
host, 197
HOSTNAME environment variable, 19
Hosts menu, 85
humount command, 140

I

ical, 80
ICMP (Internet Control Message Protocol) packets, 150
iconification, 89
ifconfig command, 173
info command, 46
InfoMagic, 8
Infomagic Web site, 192
inode, 197
insert mode, 197
installing LINUX
  boot disk, 9
  boot image, 10
  booting from floppy errors, 10
  Cylinder > 1023 message, 11
  device drivers, 11

fixing problems, 10–12
hard drive space, 9
hardware problems, 11–12
LILO (LINUX Loader), 10–11
LINUX partition types, 9
out of memory, 11
RAMdisk, 11
rescue disk, 10
space requirements, 9
swap space, 11
system gets hung up during boot, 10–11
unable to mount message, 11
Windows 95 installed after, 11
X Window System, 10
Internet, 197
  networking, 141
  querying nameservers, 148–150
  RFC (Request for Comments), 120
Internic Web site, 142, 159
I/O redirection, 197
IP (Internet Protocol), 142, 197
ISDN (Integrated System Digital Network), 197
ISP (Internet service provider), 168
ispell, 116–117

J

joe (Joe's Own Editor)
  additional features, 99
  commands, 97–98
  editing text, 96–99
  exiting, 98
  man page, 98
  non-moded editor, 97
  on-screen help, 98
  pretending it is another editor, 96
  searching for text, 98–99
  starting, 99
Joy, Bill, 104

K

kernel, 197
keyboard moving mouse cursor on-screen, 91
keyboard shortcuts, 94
kill file, 181, 197
Korn, David, 14
Korn shell, 14, 197
  setting editing modes, 18–19
  setup files, 27
ksh shell, 14, 25

L

LaTeX, 95
  ispell and, 117
lcd command, 148
less command, 20, 43
LILO (LINUX Loader), 10, 180, 197
line count, 68
line length adjustment, 64
link, 197
LINUX
  adaptability, 6
  cost, 5, 6, 7
  defining, 6
  distributions, 7
  downloading, 8
  GUI (graphical user interface), 13, 164
  interoperability, 6
  non-LINUX media and, 131
LINUX Documentation Project pages, 8
LINUX Gazette, 8, 193
LINUX International, 8
Linux Journal, 8, 193
Linux Journal Web site, 142
LINUX Resources Web site, 142, 191, 192
LINUX Speaker's Bureau, 8
LINUX User Groups, 8
LINUX newsgroups, 194
ln command, 65–66
local variables, 17
locate command, 54–55
locating files, 52–53
Lock Screen menu, 85
login directory, 197
.login file, 26
LOGNAME environment variable, 19
lpq command, 49
lpr command, 49–50
lprm command, 50
ls command, 43–44
ls -F command, 20

M

Macintosh media, working with, 137–140
magazine online resources, 193
magnifying glass, 81
MAIL environment variable, 19
mail servers, 173
MAIL shell variable, 26
man command, 46–48
man (manual) pages, 81, 197
  groff, 116
  gzipped format, 116
  joe (Joe's Own Editor), 98

maximizing windows, 89
memory errors, 12
Meta key, 198
metamail
  attachments, 127
  MIME encoded messages, 120–121
Metro-X, 77
mget command, 148
mgetty program, 178
MIME (Multipurpose Internet Mail
    Extensions), 120–121, 198
minimizing windows, 89
MIT Web site, 8
mkdir command, 14, 62–63, 164
moded editor, 104
monitor system status, 73
Motif, 76
mount command, 70–71, 198
mount filesystems, 70–71
mouse, 91–92
MouseCursor, 80
moving
  files, 45
  windows, 90
mput command, 148
MS-DOS media, working with, 132–137
Mtools
  additional commands, 136
  command-line options, 132–133
  device names, 132
  filenames, 132
  high-capacity disk format schemes, 132
  mcd command, 133
  mdel command, 134
  mdir command, 134
  minfo command, 134
  mmd command, 135
  mtype command, 135
  primary names, 132
  secondary names, 132
  VFAT (long style) filenames, 132
  wildcards, 132
  xcopy command, 135
Multimedia menu, 85
munpack, 120–121
mv command, 45

N

nameservers, 142–143
  querying, 148–150
Nation, Robert, 75
ncftp, 144

networks, 141
  accessing DNS registration information, 159–161
  automatic logins, 144–145
  Class C address, 142
  connecting to anonymous FTP servers, 143–144
  copying remote files, 151–152
  deciphering addresses, 142–143
  domain addresses, 142
  downloading files, 145–146
  executing commands remotely, 153–154
  finding route to remote host, 157–158
  hops, 158
  ICMP (Internet Control Message Protocol) packets, 150, 158
  IP (Internet Protocol) addresses, 142
  logging in remotely, 152–153, 156–157
  nameservers, 142–143
  navigating remote host, 147
  nslookup, 148–150
  ping, 150–151
  rcp, 151–152
  rlogin and rsh commands without passwords, 155–156
  rlogin command, 152–153
  rsh command, 153–154
  sending test packets, 150–151
  telnet, 156–157
  traceroute command, 157–158
  transferring files, 143–148
  uploading files, 148
  whois command, 159–161
newsgroup online resources, 193–194
newsreaders, 174
NFS (Network File System), 198
NIS (Network Information System), 198
NNTPSERVER environment variable, 174
non-LINUX media, 131
  Macintosh media, 137–140
  MS-DOS, 132–136
  UNIX files and media, 140
nslookup commands and options, 149–150

O

OLDPWD shell variable, 26
online display, 46
online documentation, 45–48
online resources, 191–193
options, 198
ownership, changing, 59

P

Pacific High Tech, 8
Pager, 77
pages, print formatted, 51
PAP (Password Authentication Protocol), 198
parent directory, 198
partitioning, 198
passwd command, 71
passwords, 71
PATH environment variable, 19
pathnames, 23
patterns within files, 53–54
periodic events, 39–40
permissions, 57–58, 198
Pico, 96, 100–101
pine, 120
  attachments, 129
  context-sensitive help, 129
  default printer, 128
  elm and, 129
  e-mail management, 127–129
  exiting, 127
  INBOX folder, 128
  metamail attachments, 127
  printing messages, 128
  reading messages, 128
  saving messages, 128
  sending messages, 128–129
ping, 150–151
pipeline, 21
pipes, 21, 198
plan, 80
POP (Post Office Protocol), 120, 173, 198
popclient, 130
POSIX, 6, 198
PostScript files, 48–49, 80, 198
PPP (Point-to-Point Protocol), 120, 198
  chat program, 170–172
  connection, 169
  ifconfig command, 173
  ISP (Internet service provider) connection, 168
  mail servers, 173
  making connection, 174
  nameservers, 174
  newsreaders, 174
  parameters, 169–170
  phone number and login sequence, 175
  pppd command, 172–173, 175–177
  ppp-off script, 174
  ppp-on script, 174
  route command, 173
  su command, 174

pppd command, 172–173, 174– 178
pr command, 51
Preferences menu, 85–86
print queue, 49
print requests, 49–50
printing, 48–51
    examining queue, 49
    formatting files and pages, 51
    PostScript files, 48–49
    print requests, 49–50
    removing queued jobs, 50
process, 198
programs
    files associated with, 21–23
    Games menu, 84
    Multimedia menu, 85
    Preferences menu, 85–86
    screensavers, 86
    System Utilities menu, 86–87
    Utilities menu, 87
    Window Operations menu, 88
    X Window System, 79–82
prompt command, 148, 199
ps command, 71–73
pull-down menus, 83–88
put command, 148
pwd command, 14, 63
PWD shell variable, 26

R

RAMdisk, 11
rcp, 151–152
Red Hat LINUX, 7
    /etc/rc.d directory, 184
    /etc/sysconfig/network-scripts file, 175
    keyboard shortcuts, 94
    TheNextLevel, 76
    /usr/doc/ppp-2.2.0f-3/scripts folder, 174
Red Hat Web site, 192
redirection, 21–23, 199
reexecuting commands, 15
regular expressions, 187–189, 199
remote e-mail access, 129–130
rescue disk, 10
resizing windows, 90
RFC (Request for Comments), 120
rlogin command, 152–153, 155–156
rm command, 66–67
rmdir command, 14
root, 199
root directory, 199
root window, 79
route command, 173, 199
rsh command, 153–156

RTS (Request To Send), 199
run levels, 180–181
    adding new start or kill file, 181
    changing, 181–183
    setting up files in directories, 183
    system, 184–185

S

save-the-world video game, 80
SCC's LINUX resources page, 8
scheduled jobs, 180
schedules and timed events
    displaying calendars, 38–39
    periodic events, 39–40
    scheduling, 37–38
scheduling events, 37–38
screen editor, 199
screens, virtual size, 77
Screensaver menu, 86
screensavers, 86
script, 199
search path, 199
searching and replacing text
        with vi, 106–107
searching for text
    joe (Joe's Own Editor), 98–99
    vi, 108–109
sendmail, 120
serial ports for user login, 178–179
servers, 77–76, 199
shadow passwords, 168
shell aliases, 16–17
shell commands, 24–25
SHELL environment variable, 19
shell script, 199
shell variables, 25–26
    references, 15
    setting to environment variables, 25
shells, 13, 199
    BASH (Bourne Again SHell), 14
    command line editing, 18–19
    ksh, 14
    leaving, 68–69
    setting editing modes, 18–19
shutdown command, 179
single character quoting, 15
single quotes (') string quoting, 15
Slackware, 7
Slackware Web site, 192
sloppy focus method, 78
smail, 120
smart host, 173
SMTP (Simple Mail Transfer Protocol),
        120, 199

sort command, 55–56
sorting and searching data, 52–56
sorting data, 55–56
sound programs, 85
special characters, 26–27
spell-checking text, 116–117
SSC Web site, 114
ssh command, 153
Stallman, Richard M., 102
standard environment variables, 19–20
StarOffice, 95
starting, 180
start file, 181
startup files, 27
stderr file, 21–23
stdin file, 21–23
stdout file, 21–23
sticking/unsticking windows, 90–91
sticky windows, 78
storing information, 25–26
string character quoting, 15
strings, 187–188
stty command, 26
su command, 72–73, 174
Sunsite Web site, 8, 143, 192
super user, 199
S.U.S.E. LINUX Web site, 192
switching tasks, 93
symbolic link, 199
system, 68–74
  changing identity, 72–73
  changing password, 71
  checking on, 71–72
  checking on users, 69–70
  leaving shell, 68–69
  monitoring system status, 73
  mounting filesystems, 70–71
  user and system status, 73–74
system administration, 163–165
  deleting users, 165
  finding system files, 166
  networking with PPP (Point-to-Point
    Protocol), 168–178
  run levels, 180–181
  scheduled jobs, 180
  serial ports for user login, 178–179
  shutting down LINUX, 179
  starting LINUX, 180
  user control file management, 167–168
system administrator, 199
system files, 166
system run levels, 184–185
system status monitor, 73
System Utilities menu, 86–87
System V UNIX, 6

T

tail command, 67
tar archives, 33–34
tar command, 33–34
Task Bar, 79
tasks, switching, 93
Taylor, Dave, 122
TCP (Transmisson Control Protocol), 199
tcsh, 200
telnet, 156–157, 200
TERM environment variable, 19
terminal displaying settings, 26
terminal windows, 81, 85
TeX and ispell, 117
text, 95
  editing, 96–114
  Emacs editing, 102–104
  formatting, 114–116
  inserting external, 105
  joe (Joe's Own Editor), 96–99
  Pico editing, 100–101
  searching and replacing, 106–107
  searching for, 108–109
  spell-checking, 116–117
  vi editing, 104–114
  wrapping lines, 112–114
text editors, 95
  choosing, 96
  Emacs, 96, 102–104
  joe (Joe's Own Editor), 96–99
  Pico, 96, 100–101
  vi, 96
text formatter, 200
TheNextLevel, 83–88
tilde (~) abbreviation for home
    directory, 20
top command, 73
Torvalds, Linus, 6
traceroute command, 157–158
troff, 114

U

umask command, 59–60
unable to access the CD or disk drive
    message, 11
unable to mount message, 11
unalias command, 17
UNIX files and media, 140
unzip archives, 37
unzip command, 36–37
uploading files, 148
Usenet, 200
user and system status, 73–74

user control file management, 167–168
user name, 200
users
  adding, 164
  checking on, 69–70
  deleting, 165
  serial ports for login, 178–179
/usr/doc command, 48
utilities, 86, 200
Utilities menu, 87
UUCP (UNIX to UNIX Communications
    Program), 200
uudecode command, 35–36
uuencode command, 34–35
uuencoded file, 200

V

vi mode, 15, 18–19
vi (visual editor), 96, 104, 200
  command mode, 104
  commands with repeat count, 114
  defining modes, 104
  deleting text, 104–105
  editing commands, 19
  editing text, 104–114
  exiting, 105
  fmt and, 114
  input mode, 104, 110–111
  inserting external text, 105
  matching parentheses, brackets, and
      braces, 111
  moded editor, 104
  modes, 96
  operators and objects, 111–112
  repeating commands, 106
  saving settings, 108
  searching and replacing text, 106–107
  searching for text, 108–109
  setting options, 109–110
  small file size of, 96
  starting, 110
  status line, 110
  undoing changes, 106
  UNIX/LINUX tools and, 96
  wrapping text lines, 112–114
video programs, 85
virtual console, 81
virtual memory, 200

W

w command, 73–74
wc command, 68
whitespace, 25

whois command, 159–161
whois help command, 160
wildcard, 200
window manager, 200
  modifying characteristics, 85–86
  taking action on client window, 87–88
Window Operations menu, 87–88
windows, 89–91
Windows 95 installed after LINUX, 11
word count, 68
words, 24–25
working directory, 200

X

X server, 200
X Window System, 10, 75, 200
  client, 76
  exiting, 88
  FVWM, 76
  managing windows, 76
  Motif, 76
  mouse, 91–92
  programs, 79–82
  servers, 76–77
  starting, 92–93
  window managers, 76
xbill, 80
xcalc, 80
xearth, 79
xeyes, 80
xfishtank, 79
XFree86, 76
xload, 78
xmag, 81
xman, 81
xsnow, 79
xterm, 81–82
xv, 82
xvscan, 82
xwd, 82

Z

zcat command, 36
zcmp command, 33
zdiff command, 33
zgrep command, 33
zip archives, 36–37
zip command, 36–37
zless command, 33
zsh shell, 200
  environment variables, 25

IDG BOOKS WORLDWIDE
BOOK REGISTRATION

Register This Book and Win!

We want to hear from you!

Visit **http://my2cents.dummies.com** to register this book and tell us how you liked it!

- ✔ Get entered in our monthly prize giveaway.

- ✔ Give us feedback about this book — tell us what you like best, what you like least, or maybe what you'd like to ask the author and us to change!

- ✔ Let us know any other *...For Dummies* topics that interest you.

Your feedback helps us determine what books to publish, tells us what coverage to add as we revise our books, and lets us know whether we're meeting your needs as a *...For Dummies* reader. You're our most valuable resource, and what you have to say is important to us!

Not on the Web yet? It's easy to get started with *Dummies 101*®: *The Internet For Windows*® *95* or *The Internet For Dummies*®, 4th Edition, at local retailers everywhere.

Or let us know what you think by sending us a letter at the following address:

...For Dummies Book Registration
Dummies Press
7260 Shadeland Station, Suite 100
Indianapolis, IN 46256
Fax 317-596-5498

BUSINESS AND
GENERAL
REFERENCE
BOOK SERIES
FROM IDG

COMPUTER
BOOK SERIES
FROM IDG